SURVIVING

DENALI

A Study of
Accidents on Mount McKinley
1910-1982

by JONATHAN WATERMAN

THE AMERICAN ALPINE CLUB
NEW YORK

Library of Congress Catalog Number 83-072260
ISBN 0-930410-18-1

Manufactured in the United States of America

Published by The American Alpine Club, Inc.,
113 East 90th Street, New York, New York 10128

The American Alpine Club, founded in 1902, is a
public foundation supported by concerned alpinists.
It is dedicated to the exploration and study of high
mountain elevations and the polar regions, the
cultivation of mountaincraft, and the promotion and
dissemination of knowledge pertaining to mountains
and mountaineering.

Design: Kay Susmann

Graphs: Nancy Young

Photo Credits:
Scott Gill, pp. 2-3 (*Denali from the North*),
pp. 4-5 (*Crossing the McKinley River*), pp. 52-53,
122-23; Glenn Randall, pp. 6-7; Roger Robinson,
pp. 70-71, 152-53; Jonathan Waterman, pp. 20-21,
36-37, 88-89, 108-9, 138-39.

Permission to reprint copyrighted material is
acknowledged: p. 21, © Howard N. Snyder 1973;
p. 153, © The Mountaineers 1977.

To Chris and his courage

WHY DENALI?

The State of Alaska Board of Geographic Names now refers to Mount McKinley as *Denali,* the original Indian name for the peak, which means *The High One.* In 1896, a prospector, ignorant of native traditions, named the mountain for William McKinley, the Republican presidential candidate of the day. The Federal Government still retains the name *Mount McKinley,* although the National Park lands which encompass the mountain were renamed *Denali National Park and Preserve* in 1980. Except in quoted material, this book uses the name *Denali* throughout.

The mountain lies at latitude 63 degrees north, 390 kilometers from the Arctic Circle, and is 6,194 meters (20,320 feet) high.

ACKNOWLEDGMENTS

For all their time and invaluable perspectives, my special thanks to: Bob Gerhard, Debbie Frauson, Roger Robinson, Tom Griffiths, and Scott Gill, all of Denali National Park and Preserve.

I would also like to thank: Nancy Young for her excellent graphics; Sindy Ernst, Mike Kennedy, Tom Schwarm, Brian Okonek, Glenn Randall, Ralph Bovard, Dave Buchanan, Rod Newcomb, Bradford Washburn, and Charles S. Houston for their patient review of the manuscript and for their insights.

For generously contributing photographs, I am grateful to: Dave Buchanan, Mike Covington, Mike Graber, Scott Gill, Art Mannix, Holm Neumann, Brian Okonek, Glenn Randall, Roger Robinson, Kathy Sullivan, Jack Tackle, and Ian Wade.

And thanks to Patricia Fletcher and Franc de la Vega for their patient prompting and copy-editing.

These selfless people—rangers, climbers, guides, writers, photographers, teachers, doctors, editors, and friends—all know the meaning of service to the climbing community.

PREFACE

I welcomed the opportunity to write the preface to this much needed and essential book because I love Denali and am concerned that its rapidly growing popularity among climbers could result in a serious increase in fatal and near-fatal accidents. Due to its height, its extreme weather and its accessibility, Denali is a singularly dangerous mountain and climbers should be made aware of the problems that frequently arise.

The mountain's accessibility is enhanced both by glacier flights from Talkeetna and the fact that there are several gradual, nontechnical routes to the summit which attract less experienced mountaineers. Denali is the only major mountain in the world where simple registration with a government agency is all that is required. If an accident does occur, someone will then know where to look and who to notify. Nevertheless, it is really the climbers' responsibility to regulate themselves and to take care of each other if a mishap should occur.

The obvious goal of any mountaineering expedition is to reach the summit. However, most responsible climbers will take into consideration other priorities such as the ability to resolve their own problems, to dispose of human waste and to carry nonburnable trash back down the mountain. In other words, style and companionship should take precedence over the ultimate goal of reaching the summit.

I have led ten expeditions to Denali, nine of which reached the summit without serious mishap. Although the tenth expedition did put in a new route variation to the sixteen-thousand-foot level on the West Buttress, it turned back short of the summit because of a potentially serious medical problem involving one member of the team. The decision to descend was made before the problem became critical because I realized that our team was too small to effect its own evacuation should that become necessary. I also recognized the danger in making a decision to continue when there was a potential crisis that might involve others in a rescue attempt. When I climb, I never commit myself to reaching the summit until I am on it.

All too frequently, inconsiderate climbers, who continue despite unresolved problems, become involved in life-threatening situations higher up on the mountain. Many parties, particularly on the popular West Buttress, who do not have experienced leadership and are unable to resolve their own problems, find it necessary to call upon guides or more experienced climbers to rescue them.

If this book is read and studied prior to departure, it should help climbers to appreciate the intricacies of climbing Denali and to anticipate the dangers of storm, extreme cold and altitude-related illness before they become life threatening. The information provided should help climbers to exercise good judgment in a crisis where matters can quickly get out of hand. When I look back on my own expeditions, I am reminded of the very fine line that exists between success and disaster on Denali. I wish that a book like this one had been available to help increase that narrow margin of safety when I started guiding on Denali in 1976. *Surviving Denali* should be required reading for anyone who wants to climb the mountain.

All of us who climb Denali in the future—whether for the first time or for the eleventh time—owe a vote of thanks to the National Park Service and to the members of the climbing community who contributed to this book.

As a Denali guide, a National Park Service Ranger and an outstanding climber, Jon Waterman has firsthand knowledge of how quickly dangerous situations can develop on Denali. In 1982, he completed the second winter ascent of the mountain, via the Cassin Ridge. We are all grateful to him for this book and for the perspectives it contains.

We also owe a debt of gratitude to The American Alpine Club for making publication possible as part of its continuing effort to foster safety and to preserve the freedom of American mountaineering.

MICHAEL COVINGTON

CONTENTS

INTRODUCTION

Denali is the coldest, highest mountain in North America. Hard-core alpinists, rock climbers, mountaineers and neophyte backpackers flock from every country in the world to pit themselves against the mountain. Although most of these people succeed, too many others fail because of the cold, altitude sickness, falls, avalanches, storms, or their own negligence. Accidents on the mountain are common.

From 1973-1982, 0.5 percent of the climbers on Denali died. This figure is more than ten times the death rate in Grand Teton National Park or Mount Rainier National Park. Denali deaths are often attributed to the cold and altitude; however, inexperience and lack of knowledge are just as deadly.

Rescue costs on Denali exceed those for any other mountain rescue in the country. Although these costs are small compared to the tax money spent on searches for ships lost at sea or downed airplanes, one still wonders if climbers shouldn't take more responsibility for their accidents and expensive rescues. For instance: three Army helicopter rescues on Denali in 1982 cost the American taxpayer $67,000!

Some people have suggested that climbers post a bond to cover potential rescue costs. Others feel that an insurance program should be developed in this country that would cover the costs. Three victims have voluntarily paid for the costs of their Denali rescues through European insurance policies. Apart from these, all rescues have been paid for by U.S. government agencies regardless of the victim's individual insurance coverage.

Although helicopter rescues have undoubtedly saved many lives on Denali, the availability of "free" helicopters has encouraged both a sad lack of self-reliance and an interruption of the wilderness ethic on the mountain. This book attempts to inspire self-sufficiency and to prevent accidents, deaths and costly rescues.

Surviving Denali presents a series of accident narratives together with recommendations on how to climb the mountain. It is not a scientific or medical treatise. For those who wish further information, there is a bibliography and appendices. Of course, no book can match the judgment, skill and intuition gained from experience.

In many instances, such as when frostbite occurs, the victims either take care of themselves or are evacuated quietly by their own team. Although self-evacuations are usually not reported, they nevertheless portray the most exemplary behavior on Denali. There is considerably more documentation on the big, costly rescues in which the victims lacked the necessary experience or were not able to take care of themselves. When known, the rescue costs are noted in the summaries at the end of each chapter. In some cases, it is also noted whether the costs were paid by the rescued party. The omission of rescue costs indicates that complete information was not available. Although accidents in other areas of the Alaska Range are excluded, the text is also applicable to climbs on Mounts Foraker, Hunter, Huntington, Russell, Deborah, and Hayes.

Admittedly, reviewing accidents after the fact has its limitations, as every climber makes mistakes. There are also accidents involving objective dangers that can be attributed to just plain bad luck. Then, too, if all accidents could be prevented, it's conceivable that many climbers might lose interest. It is hoped, however, that this book will help those who come to Denali and the Alaska Range to climb with greater safety.

18

SURVIVING DENALI

1
THE SELF-SUFFICIENT PIONEERS
1910-1967

Alone, their last desperate chance now gone, the men relinquished the fragile thread of life.

Howard Snyder in
The Hall of the Mountain King

Denali was the unknown and was spoken of in hushed tones. The early climbers, who were willing to risk life and limb for North America's highest peak, were always a step away from disaster. There were no rescue teams and no helicopters; equipment was primitive and very little was known about high-altitude sickness, rope technique, avalanches or first aid. Self-sufficiency, a concept alien to many modern climbers, was tantamount to their survival.

Nearly all climbers on Denali—particularly the pioneers—have found their limits. Given the arctic cold, storms and altitude, it is easy to overextend oneself. In addition to many near misses, 5.9 percent of the early climbers were involved in accidents. This figure is more than twice the rate for recent (1967–82) climbs on Denali. In the early years, climbing Denali was considered an outstanding achievement. The mountain was unknown and had a mystique that was almost malevolent. What the early climbers lacked in knowledge and equipment, they made up for in self-sufficiency and perseverance; some paid an eternal price.

In a one-day summit bid in 1910, four plucky "sourdough" miners carried double-bit axes and a fourteen-foot spruce pole for eight thousand feet to the north summit of Denali. They made no mention of altitude sickness and considered ropes to be unnecessary. Their diet consisted of doughnuts, steaks and stew.

Three years later, Hudson Stuck, Archdeacon of the Yukon, and his party made the first ascent of the higher, south summit. The night before the attempt, they lay sleepless with indigestion. After they started up, Stuck wrote, "We were rather a sorry company. Karstens still had internal pains; Tatum and I had severe headaches. Walter was the only one feeling entirely himself." Stuck "had almost to be hauled up the last few feet, and fell unconscious for a moment upon the floor of the little snow basin that occupies the top of the mountain. . . ."

After the first ascent, no one attempted to climb the mountain for nineteen years. Then, in 1932, two parties arrived. The first, led by McKinley Park Superintendent Harry J. Liek, was brought to the Muldrow Glacier by dog sled. From here, they climbed both the north and south peaks.

The second party, the Cosmic Ray Expedition, was flown onto the lower Muldrow Glacier. Allen Carpé and Theodore Koven started up the route on skis, taking scientific light measurements. The rest of the party, Nicholas Spadavecchia, Percy Olton and Edward P. Beckwith, stayed behind. When Beckwith became ill, Spadavecchia hiked out to get help from Fairbanks.

Carpé and Koven, meanwhile, grew concerned about the others and started back down the glacier unroped. Apparently, Carpé was traveling behind Koven on foot and fell into a crevasse. When Koven returned on skis to help, he fell into the same crevasse. Although he managed to climb back out, he bled to death in the cold.

Two days later, the descending National Park Service party found Koven's body on the glacier but couldn't find Carpé's body. They set off down the glacier, hauling Koven's body with a climbing rope. A member of the party, Grant Pearson, who was unroped, fell into a crevasse shortly afterward but managed to escape with only facial lacerations.

Liek's party broke the news to Olton and the ailing Beckwith and continued down to Wonder Lake. Liek also notified the Park Rangers that Spadavecchia had apparently gotten lost; he was found at McGonagall Pass. Olton and Spadavecchia walked out with the rangers, while Beckwith was evacuated by airplane from the Muldrow Glacier. The records don't elaborate on his illness.

Although not common, crevasse falls would occur again in later years.

In 1951, Bradford Washburn pioneered the West Buttress route with the support of airdrops and blazed the easiest way for hundreds more. His painstaking photography on the mountain was to inspire numerous new routes as well.

The first reported frostbite accident occurred in 1953; this type of accident would also occur again. Andres Henning suffered frostbitten feet while carrying loads up Karstens Ridge on the Muldrow Glacier route. Although he carried insulated felt boots, he was climbing in leather boots. When his feet turned black, his party descended to McKinley River; he was then flown out to Wonder Lake by a survey helicopter. Park Ranger Elton Thayer drove Henning out of the Park.

The next year (1954), Thayer led a bold first ascent of the South Buttress. After reaching the summit, the party of four then started down the Muldrow Glacier route. In order to safeguard a steep section of Karstens Ridge, Thayer was the last man on the rope. The group was tired and snow conditions were not conducive to ice-ax belays. Thayer slipped as he skirted the ridge crest, pulling his companions nine hundred feet before one member of the group fell into a crevasse and stopped the fall. Thayer was killed and George Argus broke his hip. The two remaining climbers left Argus with all of the provisions and hiked out to Kantishna to get help.

Six days later, a helicopter dropped a seven-man rescue team at six thousand feet, the highest landing yet made on

Denali. They carried Argus on a litter to McGonagall Pass. From here, he was evacuated by helicopter. This was the first rescue team on the mountain. In time, as more climbers came, self-sufficiency was forgotten, helicopters flew higher and higher, and rescues became commonplace.

Aircraft began to play an increasingly important role on the mountain. Airplanes and helicopters have been associated with every climb since the tragic Cosmic Ray Expedition. Washburn returned and took striking aerial photographs of the mountain. However, flying near the mountain was chancy and involved more vagaries and downdrafts than the primitive crafts could handle. Wreckage soon began to litter the mountain.

In 1944, and again in 1952, military plane crashes on the glaciers east of Denali accounted for thirty-eight deaths. Fred Beckey's 1954 Northwest Buttress team— inspired by Washburn's photographs—was supported by airdrops. Their plane, however, was forced onto the Peters Glacier and was later destroyed in high winds. In 1959, Washburn's aerial photography prompted still another team to climb the central bulge of the South Face, later named the West Rib.

In these years, airplanes also played an important role in the exploration of the isolated Alaskan bush; thus, the drone of engines became an ingrained part of Denali's history. The upward thrust of aviation technology and the mountain's increasing popularity combined to pave the way for future rescues. Climbers began to carry radios in case of trouble and the National Park Service evaluated each team's experience before permission to climb was granted. In 1960, an epic air and land rescue would serve to remind climbers of just how far reaching the consequences of an accident could be.

On May 14, a four-man expedition was landed at 10,200 feet on the Kahiltna Glacier. This was a strong party with plans to make a speedy ascent of the West Buttress. Jim Whittaker, who was there with his twin brother Lou, would later be the first American to climb Everest. Peter Schoening had been on two major Himalayan trips and John Day was a rancher who had been training on fourteen-thousand-foot peaks in Colorado.

The group reached the summit in three days from their base camp. (In later years, a gain of one thousand feet of altitude per day became the yardstick for preventing altitude sickness. A few climbers, like the sourdoughs, actually beat altitude sickness by making rapid one-day ascents.) During the descent, when they were below Denali Pass, someone slipped, possibly due to altitude sickness; all four slid down four hundred feet. Day broke his leg and Schoening and Jim Whittaker were briefly knocked unconscious. Paul Crews, who was with another team, set up a tent over Day while Schoening and the Whittakers descended to 16,800 feet. They used Crews' radio to call for help and a fifty-man rescue team from Alaska, Washington and Oregon was mobilized. Meanwhile, Helga Bading, a member of Crews' party, contracted pulmonary edema at 16,400 feet.

The next day, a sled and food were airdropped at 17,200 feet and Bading was lowered to 14,200 feet where the legendary Don Sheldon made a record-breaking glacier landing and evacuated her. Farther down the mountain, an experimental helicopter made a partial crash landing on the glacier in a whiteout and a strut ripped through the cabin, narrowly missing the heads of two rescuers. On May 20, a private plane that had dropped supplies at 14,200 feet the previous day crashed and burned a short distance from Day's tent. Both the pilot and the passenger were killed.

Schoening was still dazed and suffering from frostbite and the Whittaker twins had mild frostbite; though Day's condition was stable, he needed an airlift. On the evening of the 20th, pilot Link Luckett stripped the battery, doors and all but fifteen minutes of fuel from his chopper. He then made a "controlled" crash landing at 17,200 feet. Day was loaded into the helicopter and whisked down to another plane at 10,800 feet. Luckett plucked Schoening off the next morning.

The repercussions were widespread. A group of Japanese who were in the way of the rescue were flown off the mountain. The weather, which had been cooperative, soured. Three days later, when conditions improved, Sheldon made another flight to 14,200 feet to evacuate a rescuer with pulmonary edema. (After this, unacclimated rescuers were rarely used.) The ordeal became front-page news around the country and for weeks after the rescue, climbers on the West Buttress dined on sake and airdropped food, inside abandoned Army rescue tents.

As the mountain's reputation grew, its mystique began to diminish, thus setting a precedent for rescues. The word got out that if you were in trouble on Denali, you could be rescued. The days of the self-reliant sourdough became ancient history. In 1960, out of twenty-four attempts, twenty-three climbers were successful. (The previous year, four out of eight climbers reached the summit.) The number of climbers began to grow as climbing North America's highest mountain was increasingly regarded as a feather in one's cap. Several guided parties tested the waters and new routes continued to be sought after. Boldness, however, exacted its toll on the mountain with the worst weather in the world; during the sixties, one out of every ten climbers on Denali was evacuated and 3.1 percent were killed.

Riccardo Cassin read Washburn's description of the greatest problem left on Denali and the photograph of the South Face was enough to convince the Himalayan veteran to lead a climbing team to the mountain. In 1961, they flew over from Italy and made the difficult first ascent of the route which was later named the Cassin Ridge.

They wore knickers, knee socks and single leather boots. Jack Canali's feet were frostbitten during a gale on the summit day. On the descent, he couldn't fit his swollen feet into his boots, so another team member sacrificed his; Canali made a painful and dangerous retreat without crampons. Two days later, Sheldon flew three of the Italians to the hospital for frostbite treatment: no toes were lost. President Kennedy cabled congratulations to Cassin for "This outstanding accomplishment under the most hazardous of conditions. . . ."

Self sufficiency was superceded by radios,
helicopters and dependence on other climbers.

On the more popular West Buttress route, frostbite became common. Sometimes, getting to the top overrode concerns of the flesh and climbers would stagger up in atrocious weather conditions. In 1960, one climber got frostbitten fingers while trying to put on his face mask in eighty-mile-per-hour winds at 19,500 feet. Two members of a Canadian group lost all of their toes on a cold summit day. A British climber cinched his crampon straps too tight while going to the summit and suffered frostbite on his big toe. (Two other members of the same group experienced snowblindness as a result of inadequate amber sunglasses.) Another climber, wearing poorly insulated boots with the laces too tight, froze his foot while approaching the summit.

In 1963, after the first ascent of the dangerous Wickersham Wall by a Canadian team, Hans Gmoser said, "I do not consider it safe and I have no desire whatsoever to repeat the climb, fully aware that it was only due to lucky circumstances that we were able successfully to complete our trip." (1964 *American Alpine Journal*.) During their descent of the West Buttress, they skied by a Rainier Guide Service group, wading in hip- to chest-deep snow. One of the clients, who was breaking trail, suffered frostbite because his feet were continually submerged in the sub-zero, beneath-the-surface snow. Thirty-three days after the Canadian Wickersham Wall climb, a Harvard team completed a more difficult route on the wall. As of 1982, neither of these routes had been repeated, probably because of the avalanche dangers.

Also in 1963, a Canadian climber got frostnip on his fingers while fixing a stove. Then, while digging a cave at 12,800 feet, his mittens got wet. Later the mittens froze and his fingers got frostbitten.

Although frostbite injuries on Denali could be attributed solely to the arctic weather conditions, there is more to the problem than that. Dehydration, poor diet, altitude sickness and summit obsessions are probably the prime causes; frequently, equipment is inadequate. That frostbite can be minimized, if not prevented, was proved by eight climbers in the winter of 1967.

30

This was a large, self-sufficient group with prior experience in the Alaska Range. All of the climbers wore white vapor barrier or "mouse" boots. Their plan was to build igloos to escape the cold and wind. Disaster struck on the third day when Jacques Batkin fell fifty feet into a crevasse and died of head and chest injuries. He had been traveling unroped, without skis or snowshoes, which might have prevented him from falling into the crevasse. Although another member of the group had fallen into the same crevasse earlier on the climb, the hole was left unwanded. Sheldon flew the body out and the group continued—albeit halfheartedly—in Batkin's memory.

Johnston, Davidson and Genet reached the summit on March 1. They bivouacked at Denali Pass where they were pinned down by high winds for the next week with little food or water. Eventually, they dug a cave and found some fuel which Johnston had cached several years before, both of which saved their lives. The rest of the team couldn't wait any longer and assumed that the trio had died in the windstorm. After the wind abated, a large air search was organized. When the three climbers did start down, their frostbite was relatively minor, a testimony to their vapor barrier boots and to their caving instincts at Denali Pass. Despite their initial protestations, Johnston, Davidson and Genet were picked up at 13,150 feet by a helicopter rescue team. Rescue teams on Denali tended to overreact and sometimes gave capable climbers a lift down the mountain whether they needed it or not. The number of rescues grew because of the compassion of the rescuers and the rapid increase in inexperienced climbers who relied on them.

Modern "pioneers" continued to find new challenges on the mountain. The East Buttress, a variant on the South Buttress and the Southeast Spur were climbed for the first time in the sixties. All of these hard new routes were completed with "style" and without accidents.

In July 1967, the largest tragedy on Denali took place. Since then, climbers have debated the real cause of the accident. One theory is that the National Park Service regulations forced two undersized groups to merge into one large one that had no real cohesiveness or leadership.

Another theory suggests that a severe windstorm was the cause of the accident.

The actual facts are hard to reconstruct because all six members of the second summit party were killed. After an unplanned bivouac at 19,500 feet, the climbers reached the summit. However, they were caught in a windstorm on their descent and all perished. A seventh member of the group, who stayed behind at 17,900 feet, was also killed. (Five months before, during the winter ascent, three more experienced climbers coped with a similar windstorm and survived.) The team leader and three others had reached the summit the previous day and had then descended safely to fifteen thousand feet on the Harper Glacier. The seven bodies remained on the mountain as a grim reminder of an inexperienced team pitted against the ferocity of an unusual windstorm.

That same year, prolific expedition man Boyd Everett, Jr. masterminded three simultaneous American ascents on the south side of the mountain: the Cassin Ridge, the South Buttress and the hardest new route on the mountain, the American Direct south face.

While rappelling the Cassin Ridge at fifteen thousand feet (on Cassin's old fixed line), Bill Phillips fell seventy feet when the old rope broke. Although his Kelty pack and hard hat cushioned the fall, he hit his ankle but thought it was only a sprain. He descended the route under his own power and walked three miles back to a landing site. X-rays later revealed that he had broken his ankle.

The South Buttress party was hit by an avalanche at 11,500 feet. When an ice serac fell from fifteen thousand feet, two of the climbers were blown off their feet and into a crevasse over one hundred feet away. Two others were carried several hundred feet down the glacier. Except for a minor rib injury, all were unhurt and walked out thirteen miles to the landing strip.

In an exemplary ascent of the hardest route on the mountain, the American Direct, all of the climbers emerged unscathed. There were no falls, no avalanches and no frostbite. As of 1982, this elegant line has not been repeated.

The 1960s marked the end of an era on Denali. Seven books covering the pioneer period of the mountain's history were written. All of the major, logical new routes had been done. Climbing grew bolder and increasingly competitive, with higher standards of excellence. Quick, alpine-style climbs replaced fixed-rope tactics and technological advances made equipment warmer and lighter. Mountaineering became popular. Ray Genet, Rainier Mountaineering, Inc. and others began to guide on Denali and the National Park Service began to require climbers to carry radios. As more and more people came, Denali began to lose its mystique. However, the mountain had not changed; as the number of climbers increased, so did the accidents.

Perhaps climbers were lulled into a false sense of security because of the possibility of rescue or by the belief that there was safety in numbers. Self-sufficiency was superseded by radios, helicopters and dependence on other climbers. All of these factors had an adverse effect, causing caution to be thrown to the winds; such behavior would have been foolhardy for the radioless, isolated pioneer climbers.

The seventies brought a tremendous influx of a new breed of climbers to Denali and the boom began.

SUMMARY: THE SELF-SUFFICIENT PIONEERS

DATE	INCIDENT	NAME	ROUTE & ELEVATION OF INCIDENT
1932	CREVASSE FALL	CARPÉ KOVEN	MULDROW 9000
1953	FROSTBITE	HENNING	MULDROW 11000
1954	CLIMBING FALL	THAYER ARGUS	MULDROW 11000
1960	CLIMBING FALL	DAY SCHOENING	W BUTTRESS 18000
1960	HAPE	BADING	W BUTTRESS 16400
1960	FROSTBITE	*	W BUTTRESS 19500
1960	FROSTBITE	2 CANADIANS	W BUTTRESS 20000
1960	FROSTBITE	*	W BUTTRESS 19000
1960	SNOW BLINDNESS	2 CLIMBERS	W BUTTRESS *
1960	FROSTBITE	*	W BUTTRESS 19500
1961	FROSTBITE	CANALI	CASSIN 19000
1963	FROSTBITE	RGS CLIENT	W BUTTRESS 11000
1967 WINTER	CREVASSE FALL	BATKIN	W BUTTRESS 7000
1967 WINTER	FROSTBITE	JOHNSTON DAVIDSON	W BUTTRESS 18200
1967 JULY	HYPOTHERMIA	CLARK JANES LUCHTERHAND MCLAUGHLIN RUSSELL S TAYLOR W TAYLOR	MULDROW 17900-19500
1967 AUGUST	AVALANCHE	4 CLIMBERS	S BUTTRESS 11500
1967 AUGUST	CLIMBNG FALL	PHILLIPS	CASSIN 15300

COMMENTS	HOW EVACUATED	RESULT
UNROPED	SLED	2 DEATHS
INADEQUATE LEATHER BOOTS	ON FOOT, HELICOPTER	*
SLIP ON DESCENT, UNFAMILIAR WITH KARSTENS RIDGE	LITTER, HELICOPTER	DEATH BROKEN HIP
RAPID ASCENT, SLIP ON DESCENT	HELICOPTER	BROKEN LEG CONCUSSION
LOWERED TO 14,200 FEET	LITTER, AIRPLANE	*
WINDY SUMMIT DAY	ON FOOT	FROSTBITE ON FINGERS
COLD SUMMIT DAY	ON FOOT	ALL TOES AMPUTATED
CRAMPON STRAPS TOO TIGHT	ON FOOT	FROSTBITE ON LARGE TOE
INADEQUATE AMBER SUNGLASSES	ON FOOT	TEMPORARY SNOWBLINDNESS
INADEQUATE BOOTS	ON FOOT	FROSTBITE ON FEET
ALPINE CLOTHING, STORMY SUMMIT DAY	ON FOOT	MILD FROSTBITE
BREAKING TRAIL WITHOUT SNOWSHOES	ON FOOT	FROSTBITE ON FEET
UNROPED	SLED	DEATH
WINDSTORM FORCED 6-DAY BIVOUAC	HELICOPTER (13150')	PARTIAL AMPUTATION 3 TOES 1 TOE AMPUTATED
WINDSTORM, INEXPERIENCE		7 DEATHS
SERAC AT 15000'	ON FOOT	1 MINOR RIB INJURY
RAPPELLING ON OLD FIXED ROPE	ON FOOT	BROKEN ANKLE

*INDICATES INFORMATION NOT AVAILABLE

2
HIGH ALTITUDE PULMONARY EDEMA

Without the rapid descent,
before the fluid buildup in my lungs
got worse, I would have been
yet another statistic on Denali.

Jonathan Waterman

On June 24, 1976, while with a group on Denali, I watched a Japanese climber lurch into the 14,200-foot West Buttress camp and collapse from exhaustion. He had climbed from seven thousand feet in four days. Later that evening, his friends came to our camp asking for a doctor; we found one in another group and then walked over to the Japanese tent.

Ten yards outside of the tent, I heard the fluid gurgling in his lungs; his pulse was 130. A Park Service climbing team at seventeen thousand feet radioed for a helicopter. Meanwhile, the victim's condition deteriorated rapidly: his pulse climbed to 140 and he lost consciousness. At midnight, with minimal light, a helicopter landed and whisked the climber off to the hospital. He made a dramatic recovery with descent.

The victim had climbed too fast for proper acclimatization. An ascent rate of one thousand feet per day might have prevented his high altitude pulmonary edema (HAPE).

Although some climbers now recommend an ascent rate of two thousand feet per day above ten thousand feet, the old, conservative rate is recommended in this book for several reasons. I have found that the incidence of HAPE on Denali without predisposing factors (carbon monoxide poisoning, respiratory infections, prior HAPE history) is: nine victims who have climbed over one thousand but under two thousand feet per day, three victims who have climbed less than one thousand feet per day and three victims who have climbed more than two thousand feet per day (few people climb over two thousand feet). Judging by the experience of many climbers, Denali's bench marks are 3,000 to 4,000 feet higher than corresponding Himalayan or Peruvian bench marks; thus, Denali must be treated as a bigger mountain than most. For instance, the condition of climbers at seventeen-thousand-foot camps on Denali sometimes deteriorates, perhaps partly from the cold. If they were at the same altitude in Nepal, it would be conducive to rest and recovery. Most climbers fly from 300 feet in Talkeetna to 7,000 feet on Denali and begin their climb with no acclimatization period for a 6,700-foot altitude differential.

Of course, many people climb two thousand feet per day on Denali with no ill effects. Because of the variance in each individual's susceptibility to the various forms of altitude sickness, it is best that climbers begin conservatively until they can gauge the rate that is safest for them.

HAPE is a form of acute mountain sickness (AMS) that is dangerous due to its rapid onset. Because HAPE isn't usually diagnosed in its early stages, it can progress to life-threatening seriousness within hours. Initial symptoms include breathlessness, an increased respiratory rate and a dry cough. AMS symptoms, such as headache, insomnia, reduced urine output, nausea, lack of appetite and peripheral edema (swelling of hands, feet and face) can all accompany HAPE. High altitude cerebral edema (HACE), AMS and HAPE all involve abnormal fluid shifts to the lungs and brain.

Three days before the evacuation of the Japanese climber, a Rainier Mountaineering, Inc. client had been unable to keep the pace set by his guides to 14,200 feet. This group had climbed from seven thousand feet in five days. On the

A body on the West Rib.

RAY GENET

sixth day, the client rested; on the seventh day, however, he contracted pulmonary edema and had to be evacuated by helicopter.

Although many people reach the 14,200-foot camp in five days from 7,000 feet with no ill effects, a rest day at 14,200 feet can often help to clear up any altitude problems. The Rainier Mountaineering client probably should have taken two more days to reach 14,200 feet, particularly as he had difficulty in keeping up with the pace of his group.

Both of these experiences provided a sobering introduction to HAPE which I thought was a *rare* high-altitude disease. As drowning in one's fluids seemed to be such a grisly fate, our group discussed the various means of preventing such an occurrence. The solution seemed simple enough: ascend an average of one thousand feet per day to acclimatize properly, drink enough liquid and avoid unnecessary exertion. In the event of headaches, nausea, or any debilitating sickness, descend immediately. We then moved our camp to 16,200 feet.

Several days later, on July 1, a Genet-Porzak guided party stopped at 16,200 feet because one of the clients was too tired to continue despite the fact that he had stayed well below the average ascent rate of a thousand feet per day and seemed to be following all the rules of acclimatization. The next night he developed HAPE and was given Lasix, a diuretic that drains fluids from the body. The guides helped him walk down to 14,200 feet where a doctor examined him. He then lapsed into unconsciousness with a frothy, bloody sputum and bubbling rales in his chest. (Rales are indicative of fluid build-up in the lungs. Heard through a stethoscope, they have been described as sounding like a lock of hair being rubbed between one's fingers next to one's ear.) His pulse rate climbed to 140 and his condition appeared to be deteriorating rapidly. The weather precluded a helicopter evacuation and two hours after reaching 14,200 feet, he died.

On July 5, when our group descended to 14,200 feet, two of the climber's friends were waiting with his body for a helicopter. Somehow, it seemed wrong that a twenty-four-year-old should lie wrapped in an American flag while six thousand feet above, on the summit, eighty people had celebrated the Bicentennial. When I learned that the victim had contracted HAPE on a previous trip, the picture gradually came into focus. I continued to learn about HAPE from the mistakes of others and, six years later, would learn as a victim.

In 1978, Galen Rowell and Ned Gillette climbed from 10,000 feet to the summit (20,320 feet) and back to 17,200 feet within twenty-four hours. The logic behind their ascent was simple: move light and fast in order to beat storms and altitude sickness. On the descent, Rowell contracted HAPE; after a night at 17,200 feet, he made a rapid descent and his condition improved. In this instance, Rowell gambled on his years of high-altitude experience and won by a slim margin. Many other world-class climbers also "race" and "beat" HAPE down the mountain. No doubt, there have been many similar cases in which climbers were not even aware that they had HAPE because they descended before the symptoms became debilitating.

Reinhold Messner went to Denali in 1976 and applied his knowledge of altitude in a twelve-hour round trip to the summit from 14,200 feet. Regardless of experience, however, many climbers underestimate Denali and go too fast.

In 1979, bad weather delayed the West German Mount McKinley expedition. After flying to the seven-thousand foot landing strip, they immediately began a rapid ascent despite an earlier warning from Park Rangers to climb slowly. Two days later, Georg Wudi developed HAPE and the party stamped out an S O S in the snow at 12,500 feet on the West Buttress. On July 1, pilot Jim Sharp saw the signal, landed at 14,200 feet and determined through a radio call that the Germans wanted a helicopter for Wudi. Sharp instructed them to move him down to eleven thousand feet, which they did in two hours with help from another party. Sharp then landed his Cessna 185 and took Wudi on board but refused to take any gear or one of the healthy Germans who wanted a flight out.

Wudi had been cautioned against fast ascents. If the

team had allowed more time for the climb, it is unlikely that he would have contracted HAPE.

The following year, 1980, another German team fell victim to the "tight schedule" syndrome. After sitting out a week of bad weather in Talkeetna, the team changed their plans from a quick ascent of the Cassin to a quick ascent of the West Buttress. On May 27, immediately after being flown to seven thousand feet, they started up. On the evening of May 31, Konrad Schuhmann became sick at 14,200 feet. The next night he began to spit blood, so the group started to descend. When Schuhmann failed to improve after receiving a 20 mg injection of Lasix, they radioed for an evacuation.

That same night, helicopter pilot Jim Okonek picked up the semiconscious Schuhmann at 12,800 feet. Okonek thought he was the sickest climber he had seen in years of helicopter evacuations. However, at three hundred feet, in the high air pressure of Talkeetna, Schuhmann walked off the plane, declining further medical treatment.

Strong, experienced climbers such as Schuhmann can suffer from altitude sickness when storm days that keep them tentbound lead to impatience and subsequent rapid rates of ascent. Ideally, Schuhmann's group should have allowed another two days to reach 14,200 feet. Although the team was wise to begin Schuhmann's evacuation immediately, his condition deteriorated so quickly that only a helicopter rescue could save him.

In May 1981, three American speed climbers went from 7,000 feet to 14,200 feet in one day. They planned to acclimatize at 14,200 feet on the West Buttress, descend to the landing strip at 7,000 feet and then set a speed record to the summit. After the first night at 14,200 feet, one of the group began spitting up blood. All three then descended quickly before his condition became debilitating. (I saw him at ten thousand feet, moving slowly and staining the snow red.) The strongest climber did make a summit attempt from the landing strip but, after twelve hours, turned back at 17,200 feet because he felt sick.

As climbing to fourteen thousand feet in just one day is

extremely fast, it could almost be expected that someone would get HAPE. The strongest climber felt that his mistake was not spending more time acclimatizing at 14,200 feet prior to the summit attempt.

At the same time, a German team made a fast ascent of the West Buttress. They flew to 7,000 feet on May 21 and, by May 25, had climbed to 17,200 feet. During the night, Wolfgang Weinzierl suffered HAPE; knowing his limitations, however, (he had previously contracted HAPE in the Himalaya and in Peru), he descended at noon the next day. After he reached 14,200 feet, he was coughing and weak; on May 26, a Park Service patrol helped him down to 11,000 feet. As he continued down to the landing strip, his condition improved rapidly.

Weinzierl's immediate descent was an exemplary reaction to HAPE. However, as some individuals are more susceptible to HAPE than others, it is curious that Weinzierl chose to climb fast and risk HAPE after experiencing it twice before.

On the heels of Weinzierl's aborted speed climb, a five-man German group went from seven thousand feet, on May 27, to sixteen thousand feet on June 1. After their carry to 16,000 feet, one of the climbers, Karl Muck, became ill at 14,200 feet. On June 2, he had rales in both lungs; Lasix was given intramuscularly and some improvement was noted. An evacuation was then initiated. At 1:45 P.M., Muck and one healthy member of the party were brought out by helicopter. Although Muck improved considerably on the descent, he was still disoriented when he arrived in Talkeetna.

This is another example of a situation where HAPE might have been prevented if the climber had ascended an average of one thousand feet per day.

In the October 1980 issue of *Alpinismus*, Peter Habeler wrote an article about his visit to the mountain in 1980. In it he says, "Again and again, Mount McKinley is underestimated by climbers whose arrogance borders on stupidity." He was concerned about the large number of European climbers who were getting into trouble on the mountain because of unrealistic expectations and improper attitudes. Although optimism and boldness may be virtues, when climbers overestimate their abilities and underestimate Denali, accidents can occur.

Habeler, Doug Scott and Reinhold Messner all agree that, because of the thinner atmosphere over the poles of the earth, Denali is physiologically 23,000-24,000 feet, rather than 20,320. Climbing on peaks in Colorado, Mexico, Peru, Europe and even the Himalaya is not necessarily adequate preparation for Denali. In addition to the colder temperatures on Denali, the bench marks on lower latitudinal mountains are physiologically less than the corresponding bench marks on Denali. Perhaps this explains why so many climbers underestimate the mountain and contract HAPE. Denali has to be treated as a cold, Himalayan peak.

There is almost always an explanation for why climbers contract HAPE on Denali. The primary cause is improper acclimatization. This can be prevented by gradual ascents, proper fluid intake, adequate diet and avoidance of unnecessary exertion. Some people are more prone to HAPE than others and previous victims frequently experience a recurrence on Denali. At the High Latitude Research Program camp at 14,200 feet on Denali, Dr. Peter Hackett observed climbers who suffered mild pulmonary edema the morning after taking sleeping pills (respiratory depressants). In his book, *Mountain Sickness*, Hackett suggests that bronchial conditions or pneumonia can predispose climbers to HAPE.

Another factor contributing to HAPE is carbon monoxide poisoning from cooking in sealed tents. This has happened to several climbers. In July 1974, a climber at 18,200 feet became ill from carbon monoxide poisoning which led to HAPE. He was dragged to fifteen thousand feet, where he received an oxygen air drop, and eventually a helicopter evacuation. As in many cases of HAPE on Denali, oxygen can temporarily alleviate the problem; however, when the supply runs out, the victim's condition will continue to deteriorate. Descent is the only sure treatment.

In order to acclimatize more quickly, some climbers use

Diamox, which has been shown to be a respiratory stimulant for sleeping at altitude. However, this is only recommended for climbers who experience headaches, insomnia, lack of appetite, nausea or lassitude (all symptoms of AMS) despite having followed acclimatization procedures. Diamox does not always prevent acute mountain sickness and does have undesirable side effects. It has never been shown to prevent HAPE or HACE.

Most cases of HAPE occur during the ascent of Denali. Reported cases account for fourteen percent of the total accidents on the mountain. There have been three deaths and twenty-four HAPE victims have been evacuated by aircraft. At least that many victims have descended under their own power before the symptoms immobilized them.

Although prevention is the best cure for HAPE, there is one effective treatment: immediate descent. There is nothing to be gained by waiting for helicopters that may be delayed by weather and mechanical breakdowns. Altitude, cold and high winds will only accelerate the chances of death, whereas rapid descent can save the life of someone who is suffering from HAPE as well as prevent a pilot from risking his life in a rescue attempt.

In May 1980, Mark Cupps, a client in a Fantasy Ridge trip led by Michael Covington, collapsed with HAPE at 19,850 feet on the South Buttress while the group was making their second carry to the summit. Covington alerted a pilot but was told that a helicopter evacuation was not possible at that altitude. Covington immediately started to move Cupps to a lower altitude, while the pilot tried to find a helicopter to meet them at sixteen thousand feet on the South Buttress. Five hours later, at sixteen thousand feet, Cupps' condition had improved but he still wanted to be evacuated. However, darkness prevented an Army helicopter from landing on the mountain that night.

The next morning, the helicopter broke down in Talkeetna, which meant a six-hour delay in the evacuation. Because of increasing clouds and poor visibility, Covington decided that descent was the best option, despite Cupps' insistence that he be rescued. As waiting for a helicopter was too risky, they descended and the rescue was called off. After reaching the glacier, Cupps' condition improved one hundred percent.

Covington's dynamic reaction to a HAPE victim should serve as an example for other climbers on the mountain. He initiated an immediate descent on his own rather than gambling on an unreliable helicopter evacuation. There have been instances where victims who waited for helicopters, instead of descending immediately, lapsed into unconsciousness. Descent is always the most practical treatment for HAPE.

My best learning experience with HAPE occurred in March 1982 at 19,600 feet on the Cassin Ridge. Two weeks earlier, I had contracted a bad chest cough; however, as it seemed to go away on the glacier, I naively disregarded the potential for HAPE. I had been above sixteen thousand feet on six previous trips and, although I had experienced AMS, I never had HAPE. Mike Young and I began by taking 250 mg of Diamox each morning; however, in the stressful conditions above sixteen thousand feet, we stopped taking it. On the other hand, Roger Mear didn't take Diamox at all and had no serious problems. Our fear of a winter storm made us climb quickly, which gave us occasional headaches and caused insomnia and lack of appetite. We drank two or three quarts of water per day. In five days, we climbed from 12,000 to 18,000 feet; on the sixth day, I experienced dizziness and had difficulty in breathing. On the morning of the seventh day, at 19,600 feet, I woke up with the frightening sensation of fluid in my lungs and a limited breathing capacity. When I stood up outside the tent, I had trouble keeping my balance and it was all I could do to get to the summit ridge at 20,120 feet. Continuing to the summit would have been foolhardy.

Walking down the West Buttress, I could take only three steps before I had to rest and fight for ten breaths. Although there was no blood or sputum, I coughed constantly. I felt overwhelmed by exhaustion and each step seemed to require an incredible effort, even when going downhill.

Before I crawled into my sleeping bag at 17,200 feet, I forced myself to eat and drink. My dry cough continued all that night. The next morning Mike told me I would die if I didn't descend. As I struggled down to 14,200 feet, I experienced the same limited breathing, as if there were a clamp on my bronchial tubes. After a night at 14,200 feet, I was able to breathe normally again. I had experienced the initial stages of HAPE and one more night at altitude probably would have finished me.

It is likely that other climbers will also become sick on committing south-face routes where one cannot simply walk back down, as on any other route. Mark Hesse, John Roskelley, Simon McCartney and others have been faced with this difficult decision. Hesse had AMS but continued up because he did not have the option of descending the steep south face. Roskelley was temporarily blinded because of a cerebral vascular hemorrhage at eighteen thousand feet, so he rappelled back down the Cassin. McCartney had severe HACE and was lowered down the Cassin because he could not continue up. Another HACE victim traversed from eighteen thousand feet on the Cassin to the West Rib and then went down to the West Buttress. In my case, we decided to continue because I could still walk and an upward battle, risking HAPE, seemed safer than an involved retreat back down the Cassin.

I made some big mistakes: I started up the route with bronchitis, which predisposed me to HAPE, I stopped taking Diamox halfway up the mountain and I climbed faster than one thousand feet per day. As is the case with many HAPE victims, the stressful conditions of the climb (the necessity of beating a winter storm) overshadowed my concern for proper acclimatization. I neglected some of the preventive measures of acclimatization and, without the rapid descent, before my problems got worse, I would have been yet another statistic on Denali.

SUMMARY: HIGH ALTITUDE PULMONARY EDEMA

DATE	NAME	ROUTE & ELEVATION OF INCIDENT	COMMENTS
7/6/74	HEGGERNESS	W BUTTRESS 18200	CARBON MONOXIDE POISONING
6/21/76	RAINIER MOUNTAINEERING	W BUTTRESS 14200	COULDN'T KEEP PACE, TOO FAST
6/24/76	WAKABAYASHI (JAPAN)	W BUTTRESS 14200	TOO FAST
7/1/76	GULEKE (GENET-PORZAK)	W BUTTRESS 16200	PREVIOUS HAPE
1978	ROWELL	W BUTTRESS 17200	TOO FAST
7/1/79	WUDI	W BUTTRESS 12500	TOO FAST
5/1/80	CUPPS (FANTASY RIDGE)	S BUTTRESS 19850	
6/1/80	SCHUHMANN	W BUTTRESS 14200	TOO FAST
5/25/81	SPEED CLIMBERS USA	W BUTTRESS 14200	TOO FAST
5/26/81	WEINZIERL	W BUTTRESS 17200	PREVIOUS HAPE, TOO FAST
6/2/81	MUCK	W BUTTRESS 14200	TOO FAST
3/6/82	WATERMAN	CASSIN 19600	BRONCHITIS PREDISPOSED, STOPPED DIAMOX, TOO FAST

HOW EVACUATED	RESULT	RESCUED BY	GOVERNMENT COST
HELICOPTER	RECOVERED	ARMY	$3000
HELICOPTER	RECOVERED	*	$3385.50
HELICOPTER	RECOVERED	WOODS AIR SERVICE	$1740.39
HELICOPTER	DEATH	WOODS AIR SERVICE	*
ON FOOT	RECOVERED		NONE
HELICOPTER	RECOVERED	JIM SHARP	* (WUDI PAID)
ON FOOT	RECOVERED	ARMY	*
HELICOPTER	RECOVERED	AKLAND HELICOPTER SERVICE	$849.06
ON FOOT	RECOVERED		NONE
ON FOOT	RECOVERED		NONE
HELICOPTER	RECOVERED	ALASKA HELICOPTERS	$2013.12 (MUCK PAID)
ON FOOT	RECOVERED		NONE

*INDICATES INFORMATION NOT AVAILABLE

3
HIGH ALTITUDE CEREBRAL EDEMA

**Ten climbers were killed
in the Park in 1980; Simon and I
were lucky to have survived.**

Bob Kandiko in
American Alpine Journal 1981

Imagine cerebral edema: fluid collects inside the brain causing constant headaches, then comes loss of balance; as the pressure continues building inside the skull, victims have also experienced apathy, hallucinations, seizures, failure of motor function, unconsciousness and, without descent, death. Two climbers have died on Denali from high altitude cerebral edema (HACE) and dozens have had close calls.

The symptoms of HACE are headaches, vomiting, lassitude, reduced urine output and, most often, loss of balance or ataxia. This loss of balance is what differentiates HACE from high altitude pulmonary edema (HAPE), although some of the same symptoms may be present in both. Also, victims of severe HAPE will often develop HACE. To check for ataxia, a loss of balance caused by a lack of oxygen in the cerebellum, one should walk on a straight line drawn in the snow, heel to toe. If the victim can't keep his balance, immediate descent is indicated. As in HAPE, oxygen will temporarily alleviate symptoms, but descent is the only sure cure. Drugs or medications must be avoided. Although it is not always possible to prevent HACE, careful monitoring of all party members can help to avoid needless loss of life and costly rescues.

On June 9, 1978, Bruce Hickson and Tom Crouch, who were with an Air Force Pararescue climbing team, were both stricken with altitude sickness at Denali Pass. Hickson had HACE and Crouch had acute mountain sickness (AMS). (Hickson had climbed Denali the previous year without experiencing any serious altitude problems.) The next day they were evacuated by an Army helicopter. The two climbers had been taking Diamox to prevent altitude sickness but had stopped taking it during the second half of their trip when their supply ran out; this may have predisposed them to altitude sickness.

Five days later, on June 15, a guided team reached 14,200 feet on the West Buttress. Charles Prentice, a client, complained of a headache for the next three days but seemed to perform as well as the rest of the group while carrying loads to 16,200 feet. On the fourth day, Prentice lost his sleeping bag; he then borrowed a bivouac sack. When the group reached 17,200 feet, Prentice had a bad headache. Twenty-four hours later, the weather had deteriorated and Prentice's headaches had become increasingly severe. The guide decided to take him down in the morning. However, during the night, the wind picked up and the group was forced to abandon their tents and move into igloos for the next two days.

Prentice's condition deteriorated. He became incoherent, could walk only with difficulty, and ate and drank very little; his headaches were severe and painful. He was given an hour of oxygen that was left over from a previous rescue. The guide remained with Prentice at 17,200 feet, while the rest of the group descended to 14,200 feet because the guide decided they were too weak to evacuate Prentice. The climbers tried to organize a ground rescue team but failed; they then called the National Park Service for a helicopter evacuation.

During the next two days, Prentice was unconscious at times. On the third day, a helicopter landed and evacuated both the guide and Prentice from 17,200 feet. As Prentice had slept apart from the rest of the group, the guide may not have been aware of his condition. The fate of clients who climb on Denali rests entirely on their guide's leadership and judgment. Ideally, because he had headaches, Prentice's condition should have been monitored more carefully and he should have been escorted down immediately. The guide was issued a citation by the National Park Service because he had not gotten a business permit or registered as a guide.

The following year, 1979, four Germans made the classic mistake in high-altitude adaptation when they climbed from the 7000-foot landing strip to the 16,400-foot West Buttress camp in three days. On the fourth day, they left for the summit. Valentin Demmel, Jr. and Guenter Kroh stopped at Denali Pass to camp, while Valentin Demmel, Sr. and Andreas Kahnt continued to the summit. Immediately after they reached the summit, Kahnt became seriously ill with HACE; Demmel had to carry him most of the way down. The pair took ten hours to return to Denali Pass.

Meanwhile, Kroh and Demmel Jr. had become alarmed at their partners' prolonged absence. Kroh, who was suffering from altitude sickness, descended to 17,200 feet to get help. The Mountain Travel group he met there moved up to Denali Pass to offer assistance. When Demmel Sr. and Kahnt returned, Kroh could see their visual distress signals at Denali Pass. He then descended to 14,200 feet and radioed out to the National Park Service requesting an evacuation.

That same day Kroh was evacuated by airplane from 14,200 feet, while Kahnt and Demmel Jr. were picked up by helicopter from Denali Pass. Demmel was examined at the hospital and released; Kahnt recovered quickly. Both Kahnt and Kroh were treated for frostbite.

The ramifications of a fast ascent are obvious. One group who saw the Germans on their summit day tried to talk them out of their attempt because they appeared to be ill prepared. Splitting up the team on a summit day is a frequent prelude to accidents on Denali. When a team is divided, it usually becomes weaker, as the smaller groups are less capable of carrying out a self-evacuation should an accident occur.

Two weeks later, despite maintaining an average pace up the West Buttress, one member of the Montana Denali Expedition suffered from HACE. After a rest day at 17,200 feet, James Krudener and his partner started for the summit. Krudener returned an hour later complaining of dizziness and went to sleep. During the night, his condition worsened and he developed bad headaches. The next day, he seemed a little better and could walk. On the descent, however, he was disoriented and his condition deteriorated again. At sixteen thousand feet, he had to be partly lowered down the fixed lines.

A doctor with Ray Genet's party treated Krudener at the 14,200-foot camp. Although he gave Krudener fluids, his condition did not improve; the next morning he became incoherent and could not drink. The doctor suspected HACE and dehydration. He gave Krudener some oxygen and Lasix. That morning, Krudener had a seizure and, at one point, stopped breathing.

Cliff Hudson was notified in the afternoon and, shortly afterwards, landed his plane at 14,200 feet and evacuated Krudener to the hospital in Anchorage. That night the hospital reported that Krudener was in critical but stable condition.

Unless Krudener had not been eating and drinking properly, he is an example of a climber who contracts HACE despite proper preventive maintenance. Had Krudener remained another day at 17,200 feet, it is unlikely that he would have survived.

It is probable that a third climber suffered from HACE in June 1979. However, the information received was limited due to the language barrier imposed during an interview with the Japanese climbers. A four-man Japanese expedition fixed ropes from 12,000 to 16,000 feet, up fifty pitches of rock, on a new Southwest Face route. They placed no camps on the face and, on June 27, made a sixteen-hour, continuous summit bid from twelve thousand feet! Their high point was 16,500 feet, where all four members contracted AMS. In the afternoon, Mitsuyasu Hamatani became very sick, so the leader radioed out that he "would die tonight" if he were not rescued.

A day later, Hamatani was evacuated from the face in an unprecedented high-altitude winching operation on Denali. The other three climbers traversed down to the West Rib route. Hamatani was flown to Providence Hospital in Anchorage and was released several hours later in "good condition." It is possible that Hamatani's HACE was overlooked at the hospital, since edema victims often recover very rapidly upon descent. Although the analysis in the 1980 *Accidents in North American Mountaineering* reported that there was "no apparent need for rescue," the team, which had been to high altitude in the Himalaya, told a Japanese interpreter in Anchorage that Hamatani had HACE. (This is not difficult for experienced altitude climbers to diagnose.)

The Japanese team's climbing style may have been a bit presumptuous for Denali. A summit bid, with one intermediate camp between 12,000 and 20,000 feet, is an unlikely proposition. All of the team had altitude sickness, which seems to verify the fact that they had climbed too fast in sixteen hours. As has been the case with many other climbers in a jam on Denali, safety outweighed esthetics during their retreat and nearly four thousand feet of fixed line remained to litter the route.

A year later, in 1980, the prophetically self-named "Too Loose" expedition chose to do the Southwest Face in an esthetically impeccable style: fast and light, with no fixed ropes, which also proved their undoing. Jack Roberts and Simon McCartney ran out of food at sixteen thousand feet but, with the technical difficulties behind them, they decided to go for the top. They eventually traversed to the Cassin route and two days later, at 19,200 feet, McCartney contracted HACE. When two other climbers on the Cassin, Mike Helms and Bob Kandiko, discovered them, they had been without food or water for four days. This probably predisposed McCartney to altitude sickness and Roberts to frostbite.

An example of how difficult a rescue on technical terrain can be is well defined in Bob Kandiko's account from the 1981 *American Alpine Journal*:

Try to imagine the scene: Four climbers, one who is semi-conscious, try to sort out what is left of their brains in an attempt to save each others' lives. Jack, who has assisted in big-wall rescues in Yosemite, believes a winch and cable can be dropped on the crest above. Simon can be hauled up the south face and then an air evacuation can transport him off the mountain. Mike, who is trained in mountain rescue, believes a party from the West Buttress can trudge over the summit and carry Simon over and down the tourist route. Simon mutters something about a helicopter plucking us directly off the ridge. I sit totally befuddled while dishing out the soup. So much for rational thought at 19,500 feet.

A decision is made: Mike, who is familiar with the West Buttress from previous trips, will take frostbitten Jack over while I stay to nurse Simon. Once they reach a group with a radio (we had no radio because it saved weight), a rescue can be coordinated. Surely this will take just a couple days. After all, this is Mount McKinley where rescues are commonplace!

From this point (called Day 1) Mike's and my stories are distinctly separate but ultimately integrated as we struggle to get off the mountain. Without radios we have no knowledge of the decisions being made on the opposite side of McKinley. The ensuing account reveals the astonishing sequence of events that bring us down Mount McKinley.

Day 1: Simon spends a fitful day passing in and out of consciousness. I give him a cup of soup or tea every hour. As night approaches I curl up next to him to transfer body heat.

Mike and Jack summit in four hours and trudge down to Denali Pass where they find a Mountain Trip expedition camped. Due to harsh atmospheric conditions, radio contact is impossible from Denali Pass.

Day 2: Simon's temperature returns to normal as the soup is finished and the remaining tea is kicked over; we have no food left. An irritating groin rash causes Simon severe pain until a skin ointment is salvaged from the first-aid kit.

Mike and Jack are tent-bound due to high winds and poor visibility. Still no radio contact about Simon's condition has reached the Park Service.

Day 3: Simon and I decide to try for the summit crest to save ourselves. As we begin to pack, two starved and frostbitten Scottish climbers appear on their way to the summit. They are too exhausted and ill to lend assistance but their footsteps should aid in our attempt. An hour later Simon and I rope up and begin our ascent. In two hours we travel barely a quarter mile as Simon cannot maintain his balance and is too weak to stand. We retrace our steps and erect the tent. Hot water is served for dinner.

Mike and Jack descend to 17,200 feet and locate a radio. The message detailing Simon's condition is received by Frances Randall at Kahiltna airstrip at three P.M. The Mountain Trip expedition from Denali Pass leaves for the summit.

Day 4: Simon and I have been awake most of the night using the stove to heat ourselves. It is crucial that we descend. We repack the gear, swallow Dexedrines for breakfast, and begin the arduous descent of the Cassin Ridge. Simon glissades on his seat while I belay, then I walk down. The clouds move in as a plane engine is heard. In poor visibility the plane signals it has seen us as we struggle onto a snow arête at 18,300 feet. We believe a rescue by helicopter now has been initiated. I stamp out the word "rescue" in the snow and we set up the tent and begin another wait. . . .

Day 5: No rescue has arrived. This is my fourth day without food while Simon has had one meal in the last six days. Our feeling of isolation and subsequent depression are acute. Tomorrow we will continue down. We resort to "toothpaste soup" in hopes of retarding our dehydration. This *soup de jour* causes indigestion but serves as an excellent decongestant. . . .

On a fly-by Doug Geeting and Park Ranger [Roger Robinson] spotted Simon and me descending the Cassin Ridge. We appeared tired but capable of moving so no rescue has been organized. Our crucial food shortage was obviously not emphasized through radio contact.

Day 6: Simon and I get motivated by Dexedrines and stumble down to an old campsite at 17,000 feet. The last gallon of fuel is retrieved from the cache and used tea bags are extricated from the snow. Above the campsite two coils of climbing rope are miraculously discovered. These will be used in rappelling the

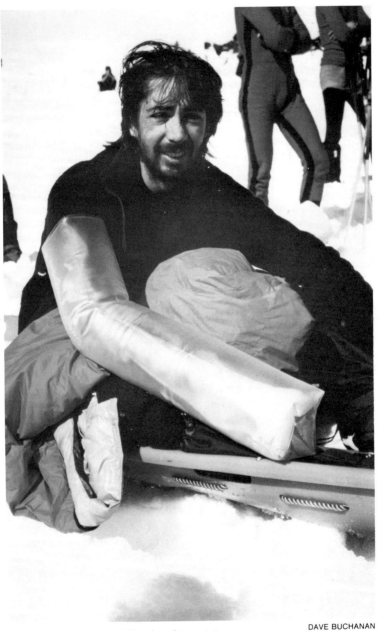

DAVE BUCHANAN

Simon McCartney at the landing strip
after his rescue from the Cassin Ridge.

upper rock band. The diluted tea created optimism on my fifth day without food.

Heavy snows and high winds prevent a rescue attempt from the West Buttress.

Day 7: Barely able to stand, Simon and I begin the rappels. Frustration results in tears as we struggle to find anchors in the rock. Halfway through the rockband we spot four climbers erecting a tent on the slope below. As luck would have it, the ropes get caught on the next rappel. We are too weak to jumar up to unhook the snag and so we continue down with only one rope. Six hours after leaving 17,000 feet we collapse into the climbers' arms. . . .

Day 8: In the company of the four Pennsylvania climbers, Simon and I rappel the lower rockband just in time to catch a Japanese party which is also retreating after an unsuccessful attempt on the Cassin. They have a radio and call Frances Randall indicating that we are alive but in desperate need of food. She contacts the park rangers who are about to leave Talkeetna to evacuate Wolfgang. Within an hour a food-drop is made on the hanging glacier at 14,200 feet and Wolfgang is on his way to Anchorage. Jack is flown out from the glacier by Geeting and is taken to Anchorage hospital for frostbite treatment.

Day 9: Simon and I descend the ice arête with the inexperienced and frightened Pennsylvanians who use pitons for brake bars and want to rappel the arête instead of moving along the new fixed line. We finally reach the glacier at the base of the Japanese Couloir. Simon has contracted severe trench foot and can barely walk.

Day 10: In white-out conditions Simon and I follow faint footsteps down the northeast fork. In the upper icefall we encounter a steep icy slope. I start down on belay only to slip and begin somersaulting. Simon is pulled off his stance. Incredibly I post-hole a leg which stops my fall. The rope jerks tight as Simon freefalls 50 feet into a crevasse. Now he is completely incapacitated with a broken wrist and a severe concussion. Fortunately the trailing Japanese party and a Minneapolis group camped below extricate Simon from the lower lip of the crevasse. Simon is carried to their camp where another radio message is made.

Day 11: The Minneapolis group generously shares its food with us as the clouds move in to prevent the authorized helicopter rescue.

Day 12: After two days of waiting at the junction of the northeast fork, Ranger Dave Buchanan convinces two Swiss mountain guides to accompany him up the glacier to haul Simon down in a toboggan. At 8:30 P.M. Simon is enclosed in a bivy sac, tied onto the rescue sled, and the long trip to the airstrip is started. With the help of twenty climbers from Kahiltna airstrip, Simon reaches the southeast fork at four A.M. When the clouds finally part at eleven A.M., Geeting zips in and flies Simon and two frostbite victims directly to Anchorage.

Again, McCartney's altitude sickness and Roberts' frostbite were due to a lack of food and water during their rapid climb. (Also, McCartney contracted immersion [trench] foot because he never took off his boots during the climb.) This rescue illustrates the slim chances of a helicopter evacuation from a route like the Cassin. Climbers on technical routes, particularly when they are without radios, must be prepared to evacuate themselves before altitude compounds the situation.

John Roskelley, the most accomplished American climber in the Himalaya, fell victim to a cerebral vascular hemorrhage (or cortical blindness) in 1981 while attempting a quick ascent of the Cassin Ridge. Roskelley and his partner, Jeff Duenwald, had climbed up to eighteen thousand feet in three days. A lack of carbon dioxide causes this seldom diagnosed problem which made Roskelley periodically blind. (During 1982–83, Dr. Peter Hackett examined five victims who had lost their vision at 14,200 feet.) Fortunately, they dealt with the situation by making an exemplary and immediate retreat. The summit was close but descent was the only cure. They rappelled back down the Cassin Ridge, utilizing numerous fixed pieces of protection. Roskelley felt that he had underestimated the mountain. Future climbers on Denali would do well to take note of his experience, because he is one of the best high-altitude climbers in the world.

A technique that is gaining popularity among climbers

wishing to prevent altitude sickness on fast, alpine-style ascents is to climb high on the West Buttress route and acclimatize before attempting a fast ascent on another route. Rapid, unacclimatized ascents have few advantages when one considers how many good climbers have contracted high-altitude sickness in this way.

On June 12, 1980, three Czech climbers left 16,100 feet on the Harper Glacier for the summit. A fourth member, Jiri Novotny, was not feeling well and stayed behind at the 16,100-foot camp. At 19,300 feet, the climbers passed the bodies of two Germans who had sat down and died in a storm two weeks before. Of the three, only Jan Mikeska remembered seeing the bodies. Later, two of the Czechs had an experience that was probably very similar to that of the two Germans.

Dan Navratil and Jan Matus were extremely weak and felt that they could not continue to the top. They decided that Mikeska should continue alone and that Matus and Navratil would descend and wait for him at Denali Pass. They did not realize that they were unroped and, on the descent, lost sight of one another; both sat down to sleep.

Another climber, Peter Habeler, discovered Matus fifty feet below the bodies of the German climbers. He was sitting in the snow with his gloves off; Navratil was discovered higher up. Within forty-five minutes, Habeler had descended to 14,200 feet to radio for a helicopter. Unfortunately, none of the radios could transmit out that day, so Habeler's companions dragged the two Czechs down to Denali Pass.

At the pass, they were attended to by an Alaskan climber, Doug Billman, until an Army helicopter was able to land that night and evacuate the two rapidly deteriorating Czechs.

Meanwhile, Mikeska had descended from the summit to the 16,100-foot camp on the Harper Glacier; he was oblivious of Matus' and Navratil's problems at the pass. The fourth climber, Novotny, was very ill, possibly from HACE. Novotny died on June 17; the exact cause of his death is unknown. They had been taking antibiotics because they thought this might prevent altitude sickness. Dr. Charles Houston feels that, "Abuse of antibiotics has gotten quite serious." There is no evidence that antibiotics can prevent altitude sickness and it is probable that the antibiotics, or some other predisposing factor such as respiratory infection, sleeping pills or carbon monoxide poisoning, had an adverse effect on the three Czech climbers. In the instance of respiratory infection at altitude, antibiotics are useless. As in other cases, altitude impaired their judgment and led to poor decision making when the group split apart three separate times.

On June 22, 1981, a group from the North Cascades Alpine School reached the summit and returned to 17,200 feet on the West Buttress. One client was exhausted and, without telling the guides, he took 60 mgs of codeine sulfate and 30 mgs of Dalmane (sleeping pills). The next day the client had HACE and could barely stand; he was immediately lowered to 14,200 feet by the guides, Alan Kearney and Tim Boyer. The guides saved his life by their quick reaction to the problem. This client, like the Czech climbers, compounded or invited HACE by his indiscriminate use of drugs.

Two months later, on August 8, another drug-related HACE incident occurred, this time to a Japanese climber, Yasuhiro Mitsuka. He had moved up the West Buttress at an average pace and, on the fourth morning at 11,800 feet, became quite ill with a fever of 100°F. His condition deteriorated that afternoon and he was given two 500 mg doses of Keflex (antibiotic) that evening. Although his condition improved briefly, he lapsed into unconsciousness at 9:30 P.M.

He died the next morning as he was being dragged to eleven thousand feet. Later, an autopsy determined that the cause of death was HACE. As the climbers had been cooking in Mitsuka's tent to keep it warm, it is possible that carbon monoxide poisoning, or the Keflex, compounded Mitsuka's sickness. Unless there is an infection present, which sometimes occurs with HAPE, antibiotics must be avoided. (The second HACE fatality on the mountain, which occurred in 1974, also involved a Japanese climber who died at 12,500 feet; details are lacking.)

On May 18, 1982, during the second ascent of the Northwest Buttress, a Mountain Trip client, John Stolpman, began to experience HACE symptoms at eighteen thousand feet, after an average ascent rate of twelve days. He suffered from loss of coordination and extreme lassitude. He was given the ataxia test and could not walk a straight line.

The guide radioed Dr. Peter Hackett at the 14,200-foot camp for advice. Hackett recommended that Stolpman take Diamox and receive an oxygen airdrop and that a ground rescue team assist.

At 10:30 the next morning, the guide reported that Stolpman's condition had deteriorated. Oxygen was airdropped and a rescue team started over from 17,200 feet on the West Buttress. At some point, the guide let two clients climb to the North Peak while he was evacuating Stolpman. When the oxygen regulator froze, Stolpman's condition began to deteriorate rapidly and he took numerous falls without self-arresting. After the rescue team reached the party, they fixed one thousand feet of rope and helped Stolpman down. He was given more oxygen and his condition improved when he reached 17,200 feet on the West Buttress.

The following day, the rescue team assisted Stolpman down the West Buttress, while the guide and the rest of the party remained at 17,200 feet. Hackett felt that the use of oxygen eliminated the need for a major helicopter evacuation. As demonstrated in other cases, a client's fate rests upon the judgment of his guide. In this instance, it is curious that the guide allowed two of his clients to split apart and climb the North Peak. It is also curious that he remained at 17,200 feet while the rescue team brought his client down. Time after time on Denali, separated parties such as this have come to grief. This group was fortunate: it had support from Hackett, a rescue team, the National Park Service and Talkeetna Air Taxi.

Individual climbers can react differently to an emergency

situation such as HACE. In the cases of the Czechs, Demmel and Kroh, McCartney, Prentice and Mountain Trip, it is interesting to note that the initial sickness was considered less important than making the summit. With HACE, this attitude can be dangerous because the victim's condition may deteriorate very quickly. Parties that split up on the mountain reduce their capability should the need for a self-evacuation arise. As with HAPE, prevention of HACE consists of a one-thousand-foot-per-day ascent rate. Oxygen air-drops are unreliable because regulators can break or freeze and good flying weather is unpredictable. Even if oxygen is available, the victim's condition will usually deteriorate as soon as the supply runs out. All drugs should be regarded as suspect in the treatment of HACE. In all HACE cases, loss of balance is a key identifying factor and immediate descent is the only sure cure.

SUMMARY: HIGH ALTITUDE CEREBRAL EDEMA

DATE	NAME	ROUTE & ELEVATION OF INCIDENT	COMMENTS
6/9/78	HICKSON	W BUTTRESS 18200	STOPPED DIAMOX
6/25/78	PRENTICE	W BUTTRESS 17200	SEVERE HEADACHES LOST SLEEPING BAG, DELAYED DESCENT
6/9/79	KROH	W BUTTRESS SUMMIT	ILL-PREPARED, FAST ASCENT, PARTY SPLIT
6/23/79	KRUDENER	W BUTTRESS 17200	AVERAGE ASCENT RATE
6/28/79	HAMATANI	SW FACE 16200	FAST ASCENT
6/12/80	MATUS NAVRATIL NOVOTNY	HARPER 19300 & 16100	QUESTIONABLE DRUG USE, POOR JUDG-MENT, PARTY SPLIT
5/81	ROSKELLEY	CASSIN 18000	FAST ASCENT
6/21/81	MCCARTNEY	SW FACE 19600	FAST ASCENT, 4 DAYS WITHOUT FOOD OR WATER
6/22/81	N CASCADES ALPINE SCHOOL	W BUTTRESS 17200	INDISCRIMINATE DRUG USE
8/8/81	MITSUKA	W BUTTRESS 11800	AVERAGE ASCENT RATE
5/18/82	STOLPMAN	NW BUTTRESS 18000	PARTY SPLIT

HOW EVACUATED	RESULT	RESCUED BY	GOVERNMENT COST
HELICOPTER	RECOVERED	ARMY	*
HELICOPTER	RECOVERED	ARMY	*
HELICOPTER	RECOVERED	ARMY	$975
AIRPLANE	RECOVERED	HUDSON AIR SERVICE	NONE
HELICOPTER WINCH	RECOVERED	ARMY	$5218
HELICOPTER	FROSTBITE, ONE DEATH	ARMY & ERA, EVERGREEN HELICOPTER	$1616
ON FOOT	RECOVERED		NONE
ON FOOT, SLEDDED TO LANDING STRIP	CONCUSSION, BROKEN WRIST, IMMERSION FOOT	TALKEETNA AIR TAXI, EVERGREEN HELICOPTER	$1745.10
ON FOOT, SLEDDED TO LANDING STRIP	RECOVERED		NONE
SLEDDED TO LANDING STRIP	DEATH		NONE
ON FOOT	RECOVERED	NPS, TALKEETNA AIR TAXI	*

*INDICATES INFORMATION NOT AVAILABLE

4
FROSTBITE

Everything was cold, even our souls.
We were drawing heavily on all our
Himalayan experience just to survive
and it was a respectful pair that
finally stood on the summit ridge.

Dougal Haston in
American Alpine Journal 1977

Winter 1982: I staggered up the last one hundred yards of the Cassin Ridge in forty-below-zero temperatures. I was the classic frostbite victim: altitude sick, dehydrated and summit bound. I could feel an icy numbness on my middle toe that was accelerated by my swollen, sprained ankle. A pressure point against the seam of my inner boot eventually constricted the circulation in my middle toe.

Mike Young helped me with my pack for the last fifty feet. He had frostbite of his nose, thumbs and two toes. His appetite had dwindled because of the altitude and he had been eating poorly. Until the final two days of our climb, we had been sleeping warmly and eating and drinking enough. Roger Mear was unscathed because his appetite was good.

Our gear represented the state of the art: Gore-Tex Thinsulate suits and neoprene overboots with strapless Footfang crampons (straps can cause cold fingers and constrict circulation in the toes) on loose-fitting Kastinger plastic double boots. We wore polypropelene socks inside of coated nylon vapor barrier socks with two pairs of thick woolen socks. Our inner boots were foam "aveolite." However, gear is secondary to body maintenance. If you don't take proper care of yourself, the best equipment in the world can't prevent frostbite.

After completing our ascent of the Cassin Ridge, we hustled down the West Buttress. Two days later, frostbite blisters, or blebs, formed on Mike's big toes and on my middle toe. We walked the last miles quickly and then tried to stay off our feet while we waited a long eight days for a bush pilot.

Neither of us suffered any serious tissue damage. Dr. Mills, who examined my feet in Anchorage, diagnosed immersion foot. In recent years, because of the popularity of vapor barrier socks, Mills has seen an upsurge in immersion foot. He believes that vapor barrier socks can be a liability for climbers with unusually sweaty feet. He stressed the importance of drying one's feet every night and of taking off the vapor barrier socks. Mills also mentioned the possibility that neoprene socks might expand at altitude and thus cause circulation constriction. Add to this the possibility of peripheral edema—a swelling of the feet at altitude—and the likelihood of frostbite becomes even greater.

A common misconception is that good gear alone will prevent frostbite. Loose-fiiting double boots with overboots help but, again, the overall body maintenance is crucial. Proper fluid intake is the most important factor. Diet, proper clothing, good acclimatization, warm sleeping conditions and avoidance of bad weather summit days are also important. Most climbers who suffer from frostbite aren't victims of the cold so much as their own poor body maintenance.

On June 25, 1981, a South Buttress group, guided by Michael Covington, reached the summit. Two days later, three of their tents were destroyed by an intense storm accompanied by drifting snow. Covington then located a crevasse where the group took shelter.

One of the clients, Nick Gilman, complained of being cold and hypothermic. Covington noticed that he was shivering uncontrollably and was not wearing overboots or gaitors.

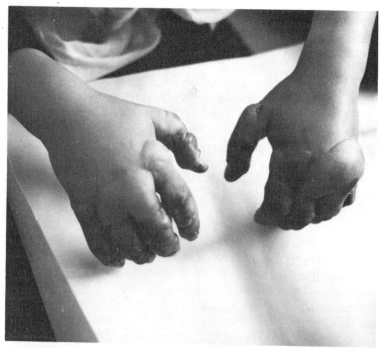

A climber's hands after thawing
at 14,200 feet on the West Buttress.

HOLM NEUMANN

Although Gilman was asked repeatedly to put on his over-boots, he never did. Covington also noticed that Gilman's boots were full of ice but, when asked about his feet, Gilman replied that they were okay. He warmed up after digging in the crevasse.

On June 28, assistant guide Steve Gall observed that Gilman was concerned about his feet and noticed that Gilman's right foot was very white. Gilman said his foot was numb but okay. The group had only slept for ten hours in a seventy-four-hour period.

The next day, when Gall told Covington about Gilman, Covington immediately checked Gilman's foot: all of his toes were black. Covington chose not to warm Gilman's foot because he didn't want to risk further tissue damage by possible refreezing. Therefore, he had Gilman sleep with his injured foot outside of his sleeping bag to prevent thawing. The next day, they dragged Gilman to the landing site on a sled. (It is important not to walk on or refreeze thawed frostbite injuries.)

Gilman was hospitalized and lost portions of his toes. Covington felt that Gilman had acted with little or no concern for his feet during most of the climb and had repeatedly ignored his warnings. The other nine members of the group, who were subjected to the same conditions, had no incidence of frostbite.

A year later, in July 1982, Akimichi Matsunaga wore only a light cap, without a hood, during his summit climb. The temperature was twenty degrees below zero and there was a twenty-mile-per-hour wind. His right ear was treated for frostbite at the thermal unit of the Providence Hospital in Anchorage.

A month later, fifty-four-year-old Miri Ercolani was trapped in a cave for three days by a windstorm at ten thousand feet on the West Buttress. Although she ate and drank adequate amounts of food and water, she never removed her plastic double boots.

When the storm ended, she continued down to the landing strip and was flown out to Talkeetna. When she removed her boots, after wearing them continuously for five days, she discovered that both big toes were badly frostbitten. She was treated in Providence Hospital.

Climbers should take their boots off every night so that they can inspect their feet, dry them and change into dry socks. Amid the various stresses imposed by solo climbs such as Ercolani's, proper care of the feet is often overlooked. This is particularly true of the harder routes, like the Cassin, because of the technical difficulties imposed, the limited retreat options and the trend towards quick, alpine-style climbing.

In July 1982, three Scottish climbers started up the Cassin without a tent. One of the group, John Murphy, lost his sleeping pad above the Japanese Couloir. Because their bottles were freezing, they drank little water above sixteen thousand feet. They never removed their inner boots, which became wet from perspiration, and wore only gaitors over their boots. On the summit day, they moved slowly because of Robin Clothier's altitude sickness. The temperature at the summit was thirty-five degrees below zero and it was calm.

The group descended to ten thousand feet on the West Buttress where Clothier and Murphy were stopped by painful frostbite blisters. They borrowed a radio but couldn't transmit to Talkeetna. Luckily, they were able to contact a helicopter rented by a *Good Morning America* television film crew who were in search of a dramatic Denali story. They were evacuated by the film crew and the timely rescue was broadcast on nationwide television. Both Clothier and Murphy were hospitalized; after the initial examination, it appeared that Clothier would lose parts of his left toes.

When I interviewed Murphy after the climb, his attitude towards the mountain was one of nonchalance. He felt that the conditions on Denali were not nearly as severe as those he was accustomed to in Scotland and that it was not nearly as cold. One could speculate that this attitude may have contributed to Murphy and Clothier suffering frostbitten feet. Climbing tentless on the Cassin was a big mistake as there are no possibilities for caving above 14,500 feet. The

Scots might have fared better if they had insulated their water bottles, removed their inner boots and not lost a sleeping pad. (In recent years, climbers have found it easier to acclimatize high on the West Buttress and then drop back to climb the Cassin. See 1982 *American Alpine Journal*, pp. 21–28.)

Many climbers, such as the Scots, who wear gaiters with no insulation in the sole of the boot, suffer from frostbitten feet. Cold can be conducted to the foot by the steel shanks in boots and crampons as well as by the below-surface snow. If you add to this altitude sickness, dehydration and lack of shelter, combined with stresses, frostbite becomes inevitable.

In May 1977, a Mountain Trip guided expedition left for the summit from seventeen thousand feet. The temperature was thirty degrees below zero. At Denali Pass, they turned back because two of the clients, Swanson and Duffy, had altitude sickness; both had been sick earlier on the mountain. Another client, Robert Larson, who wore double ski boots with gaiters and neoprene socks, had cold feet all day.

Two days later, at fourteen thousand feet, Larson's toes blistered. When a radio call for a helicopter was unsuccessful, he was helped down to ten thousand feet. Meanwhile, his frostbite blisters had thawed and the walking caused the skin to tear away. He skied the rest of the way to the landing strip. As Swanson's fingers had become frostbitten during the summit attempt, both climbers were flown out immediately.

Although air evacuation of frostbite victims is sometimes done from ten thousand feet, it's a tossup between compounding the frostbite damage further by walking out an additional nine miles or of jeopardizing the pilot. Long periods of foul weather, however, often dictate that frostbite victims either walk or be dragged to the landing strip at seven thousand feet. Many climbers simply hurry back to the landing strip before blisters develop or thawing begins and never report their frostbite.

On May 16, 1981, Alan Jennings suffered frostbitten

feet while walking to Denali Pass wearing boots and gaitors. Within two days, his feet had thawed and he walked down to 10,200 feet. An air evacuation was requested but the weather was bad for two days. On May 25, he walked to the landing strip, was flown out and admitted to Providence Hospital with frostbite on four toes.

Two weeks later, Gary Selner left for the summit from 16,500 feet on the West Rib. He began the climb with cold feet, wearing double boots and gaitors. He had constant trouble keeping his feet warm. At nineteen thousand feet, he turned back because he had difficulty staying warm in the high winds. He also knew that something was wrong with his feet. The next day, when he and his party tried to descend to fourteen thousand feet on the West Buttress, they were stopped by a whiteout. The following day, they descended to 12,500 feet.

On June 10, three days after getting frostbite, Selner had trouble descending and radioed the landing strip from eight thousand feet with a request for help. A National Park Service patrol of four, plus seven additional volunteers, dragged him to the landing strip in a sled. From here, he was flown out to Providence Hospital in Anchorage.

Selner should not have tried to reach the summit with cold feet. A recommended course of action for summit-bound climbers with cold feet is to rewarm the feet on a partner's stomach. If the feet don't warm up within an hour of leaving for the summit, it is likely that frostbite will occur.

The final diagnosis of frostbite may overlook initial, non-freezing tissue damage from immersion foot caused by vapor barrier socks. "Exposure is of many hours or days, and the result is an injury noted for its extensive edema, pain and slow recovery. . . ." (William J. Mills, Jr., M.D., *Alaska Medicine*, March 1973, p. 28.) Immersion (trench) foot may invite and compound later frostbite injury.

At midnight on June 21, 1980, a guided party left Denali Pass for the summit. The temperature on top was thirty-five degrees below zero. When they returned at 9 A.M. on June 22, one client, Wolfgang Meiers, noticed that he had

JONATHAN WATERMAN

A climber in a storm on Denali.

frostbitten all of his toes. Although his feet had felt cold during the ascent to the summit, he didn't stop to warm them. He wore double boots, gaitors and plastic bags over his feet.

Assistant guide, Nick Parker, brought Meiers down to 17,200 feet on the West Buttress, while the rest of the party continued their traverse down the Muldrow Glacier. The next day, Parker and Meiers walked down to 14,200 feet. Meiers wore vapor barrier boots to provide room for his swollen toes. During the descent, his toes broke open, making him a litter case. Parker radioed out for a helicopter but poor weather delayed the evacuation for three days. Meiers took Emperin 3 for pain and Ampicillin to prevent infection. On June 28, he was flown out from 14,200 feet. He eventually lost two toes and eight digits on his remaining toes.

Climbers who lack cold-weather experience, such as many clients on guided trips, often overlook the loss of sensation in their feet. They are seldom aware of the seriousness of frostbite and are reluctant to impose on the group by stopping to warm up their numb toes. It is possible that Meiers did not dry his feet every night, which could have contributed to the seriousness of his frostbite. The majority of the frostbite cases on Denali occur on the summit day or at a high camp where the altitude tends to affect climbers' health and make them susceptible to cold injuries.

In 1978, two Japanese climbers bivouacked at Denali Pass because they were too exhausted to return to seventeen thousand feet after their summit climb. Kohji Abe wore double boots with overboots while Koh Sato wore only double boots. Sato suffered frostbite but made it down under his own power; Abe was unscathed, probably because he wore overboots.

In 1980, members of the Boulder-Jackson expedition asked Mike McComb why he wasn't wearing overboots for his summit attempt. He replied that his "fingers got too cold when putting them on." After telling another expedition that they planned to camp as high on the mountain as they could, McComb and one other climber left in the afternoon from 17,200 feet on the West Buttress.

At nineteen thousand feet, they dug a snow trench and covered it with a tent fly. The weather turned very bad, with blinding snow, low visibility and cold temperatures. (This same night a German couple, Loibl and Huschke, sat down and died three hundred feet above McComb.) The storm continued into the morning and there was heavy spindrift inside their trench. McComb found snow in both his outer and inner boots when he put them on for the descent. He froze his feet while walking down to the 17,200-foot camp, continued descending to 14,200 feet that night and was evacuated by helicopter the following afternoon.

High-altitude bivouacs erode one's judgment and one's capacity to withstand the cold. If McComb had used overboots and slept with his boots next to his body, his frostbite might have been prevented.

In recent years, most climbers on Denali seem to prefer lightweight double plastic boots to heavier leather boots that conduct cold through their steel shanks and freeze solid when wet. In the winter of 1978, before plastic boots were available, four climbers elected to wear leather rather than vapor barrier boots on the Muldrow Glacier route.

Two separate storms below seven thousand feet ruined their tents, then an earthquake released an avalanche from the Harper Icefall that destroyed their snow cave beneath Karstens Ridge. The temperatures ranged from thirty-two degrees above zero to thirty-seven below with a constant wind. (Cold northern winds have plagued all winter expeditions on Denali.)

During a hard day of climbing from 14,500 to 15,900 feet, one of the group, Fred Barstad, overexerted himself while cutting blocks for the snow cave. He had little to eat all day and, as a result, froze his toes. He was wearing boots with overboots.

The next morning, when Barstad announced that he was going to descend, one member of the group argued with him to continue. Barstad and Dan Knight then radioed for an evacuation; after a minor crevasse fall, they began to descend. The other two climbers, Ettore Negri and Ulf Bjornberg, stayed at the high camp.

After three days of bad flying weather, Barstad and Knight were evacuated by helicopter from 9,500 feet. Meanwhile, Negri had fallen into a crevasse with a heavy pack on but managed to get out. When Negri and Bjornberg requested a flight out from McGonagall Pass, the request was denied because they weren't seriously in need of an evacuation; they then skied out to Kantishna.

Negri had superficial frostbite and lost some toenails; Barstad suffered more serious tissue damage. It is interesting to note that Barstad had no insulation in his overboots, while Negri had some. Bjornberg and Knight, who had the most insulation, suffered the least amount of frostbite. Barstad's frostbite was caused by little food, overexertion and inadequate overboots.

Only two of the six people who have climbed Denali in winter have escaped without frostbite. On the 1967 winter ascent, the team wore vapor barrier "mouse" boots. Despite being trapped for six days at 18,200 feet in fifty-below-zero temperatures, their frostbite was relatively minor. The vapor barrier boots are not rigid and impose definite limitations on any technical climbing. Crampons that are tightly strapped to these soft boots can restrict circulation and socks have to be changed regularly in order to keep one's feet dry. With only a few exceptions, however, these boots have had an excellent track record on Denali.

In 1978, a dog sledder damaged his vapor barrier boots and got frostbite on his toes at 17,200 feet. In 1980, a Boy Scout who was not eating or drinking enough suffered frostbite on his feet at 17,200 feet while wearing vapor barrier boots. In April 1982, Brian McCullough's feet were slightly frostbitten in a worn-out, leaky pair of vapor barrier boots. In June 1982, while loading an injured member of his Denali 101 team into a helicopter at 17,200 feet, Bill Ennis discovered frostbite on his toes.

The most common incidents of frostbite are those that affect the feet. This is due to the difficulty of removing boots to check circulation and initiate warming. Ears and noses are frostbitten only rarely. Fingers are only frostbitten occasionally, under unusual circumstances, because they are much easier to warm up than feet.

In June 1977, two Italian climbers spent three days on the Messner Couloir in deep snow and bad weather. (All other parties have spent only one day on this route.) Although Antonio Klingendrath's gloves were inadequate, he continued up the route in a bad storm; as a result, he suffered frostbite on his hands. The two Italians descended from 19,600 to 17,200 feet, where other climbers took care of them. Klingendrath, who refused a helicopter evacuation, was helped down to eleven thousand feet by Park Rangers; from here the two Italians continued alone to the landing strip.

In 1981, a climber descending the West Buttress, after traversing from the South Buttress, suffered frostbite on his fingers while adjusting his crampons. He also froze his toes. In 1982, during a bitterly cold April and May, I saw many climbers return to Talkeetna with frostbite blebs on their fingers and faces. One climber was a competent guide who had waited two weeks in a snow cave for the weather to clear. The selfless behavior required of good guides when dealing with inexperienced clients can be exhausting and often leads to the guides' physical and mental deterioration; this can predispose them to frostbite.

One of the most tragic frostbite victims was Barney Dennen. On June 26, 1982, he became restless in the "carnival atmosphere" of the 14,200-foot West Buttress camp and at 1 P.M. began soloing an ice slope up the West Buttress. He finished climbing the forty-five-degree ice at 8 P.M. and began walking along the ridge crest toward the West Buttress fixed line in a whiteout. He immediately broke a cornice, fell free for fifty feet and then slid five hundred feet down the north side of the ridge.

Unhurt, but exhausted, he dug a snow cave with an ice hammer while wearing only ragged silk gloves. During the fall, his pack containing mittens, windpants and a down parka had been torn away from him. A windstorm developed and spindrift avalanches swept over the entrance to the cave. His fingers became frozen and he alternately put them in his crotch and his mouth to thaw.

The next morning he climbed to the ridge crest but was forced to his hands and knees by a strong wind. He was unable to use his frostbitten hands on the fixed line, so he wrapped his arms around the rope in order to descend. His climbing partner and two members of the High Latitude Research Project (HLRP) helped him down to the heated research tent at 14,200 feet, where his hands were thawed and he was given morphine for the pain.

The next day, Dennen was helicoptered off the mountain with three injured German clients, two of whom had suffered frostbitten fingers in the same windstorm during a bivouac at 17,400 feet. Dennen spent weeks in the hospital and had most of his fingers amputated. He was nineteen and his passion in life had been rock climbing.

That crowded carnival atmosphere at 14,200 feet may have led Dennen to underestimate the mountain. An earlier start, particularly with an obvious storm building, might have offered him better odds in pursuing a pastime on Denali that is inherently dangerous; cornices, crevasses and storms give soloists little margin for error.

Boldness on Denali usually has a price. This was also true for Mark Hesse, who made a remarkable solo ascent of the South Face in May 1982, four weeks before Dennen's accident.

In 1979, Hesse's fingers had become frostbitten while he was on the Cassin Ridge. Because he had crushed his fingers in a quarter-ton press, he was predisposed to frostbite. Just before his solo climb, he helped his brother, John, up to twelve thousand feet on the West Buttress but both turned back when John developed a sore shoulder from his crutch; he was an amputee with only one leg.

Hesse spent seven and a half days on the South Face, with two open bivouacs. On the seventh day, when he was sick from the altitude, he froze his fingers. At noon the next day he reached the summit in stormy weather. He then descended to 17,200 feet on the West Buttress, where other climbers fed him. That night, someone helped carry his pack down to 14,200 feet where Dr. Peter Hackett thawed his fingers at the HLRP tent.

The next day Hesse walked down to ten thousand feet

with one of the doctors. The HLRP group and the National Park Service recommended that he ride a dog sled from ten thousand feet down to the landing strip. Hesse felt that the fifty-minute, $150 sled ride was more frightening than his solo climb.

The decision to evacuate frostbitten climbers is never an easy one to make. It takes days, even in a hospital, to evaluate the severity of a frostbite injury. On the mountain, aside from the ethical ramifications of flying out ambulatory victims, high-altitude skiplane landings are risky. Although many climbers complained about the presence of a dog-sled operation on the West Buttress that summer, it was fortunate for Hesse that he had the option of using it. Perhaps, due to the excellent medical treatment and the rapid evacuation, Hesse's frostbite did not involve tissue damage.

It is still not clear whether Hesse really needed to be evacuated. Will other frostbitten climbers, doctors or rangers cry dog sled or helicopter at the next sign of frostbite? Have climbers become less responsible with the knowledge that evacuations are possible?

In 1979, there were no research camps or dog-sled operations on the mountain. That year a climber with an old crushed finger injury walked down from the Cassin to the landing strip without bothering anyone about his frozen fingers. Frostbite is the most common and least reported accident on the mountain.

Although technological advances have made high-quality, warm clothing and equipment available to every Denali climber, frostbite continues. Rehydration, a good diet and acclimatization, together with an aggressive attitude toward the cold, are key factors in preventing frostbite. Knowledge of the circulatory system and proper dressing techniques are also helpful. If every expedition could meet an amputee—and witness the sense of loss, the frustration of a long recovery and the expensive medical bills—perhaps future climbers would understand that reaching the summit is not worth the loss of a single finger or toe.

SUMMARY: FROSTBITE

DATE	NAME	ROUTE & ELEVATION OF INCIDENT	COMMENTS
6/23/77	KLINGENDRATH	MESSNER COULOIR 18000	INADEQUATE GLOVES
3/13/78	BARSTAD	MULDROW 15900	OVEREXTENDED, LITTLE FOOD, INADEQUATE OVERBOOTS
6/2/78	SATO	W BUTTRESS 18200	BIVOUAC, NO OVERBOOTS
5/28/80	MCCOMB	W BUTTRESS 19000	BIVOUAC, NO OVERBOOTS
6/21/80	MEIERS	W BUTTRESS SUMMIT	NO OVERBOOTS
5/16/81	JENNINGS	W BUTTRESS 18200	NO OVERBOOTS
6/7/81	SELNER	W RIB 18000	NO OVERBOOTS
6/27/81	GILMAN	S BUTTRESS 15000	NO OVERBOOTS
3/6/82	YOUNG WATERMAN	CASSIN 19600	DEHYDRATION, ALTITUDE SICKNESS, INADEQUATE DIET
5/18/82	HESSE	S FACE 19000	DEHYDRATION
6/26/82	DENNEN	W BUTTRESS 16000	SOLO, CORNICE COLLAPSE, BIVOUAC, INADEQUATE CLOTHING
7/2/82	MATSUNAGA	W BUTTRESS SUMMIT	LIGHT HAT WITHOUT HOOD
7/23/82	ERCOLANI	W BUTTRESS 10000	LEFT BOOTS ON FOR 5 DAYS
8/1/82	MURPHY CLOTHIER	CASSIN SUMMIT	NO TENT, DEHYDRATION, ALTITUDE SICKNESS, GAITORS

HOW EVACUATED	RESULTED	RESCUED BY	GOVERNMENT COST
ON FOOT	FROSTBITTEN FINGERS		NONE
HELICOPTER	FROSTBITTEN TOES	NPS	$2767.20
ON FOOT	FROSTBITTEN TOES		NONE
HELICOPTER	FROSTBITTEN TOES	AKLAND HELICOP-TER SERVICE	$1767.02
HELICOPTER	AMPUTATION 2 TOES, 8 DIGITS	EVERGREEN & TALKEETNA AIR TAXI	$11439.37
ON FOOT	4 FROSTBITTEN TOES		NONE
DRAGGED TO LANDING STRIP	FROSTBITTEN TOES		NONE
DRAGGED TO LANDING STRIP	PARTIAL TOE AMPUTATION		NONE
ON FOOT	MINOR TISSUE DAMAGE		NONE
DOG SLED	MINOR TISSUE DAMAGE		NONE
HELICOPTER	AMPUTATION OF ALL FINGERS	ARMY	**
ON FOOT	FROSTBITTEN EAR		NONE
ON FOOT	FROSTBITTEN TOES		NONE
HELICOPTER	MINOR TISSUE DAMAGE, TISSUE LOSS FROM ALL LEFT-FOOT TOES	*	NONE

*INDICATES INFORMATION NOT AVAILABLE
**IN 1982, THE ARMY BILLED THE NPS $67,000 FOR ALL RESCUE OPERATIONS.

5
CLIMBING
FALLS

Perhaps it would have been
a wise decision
not to push our luck.

*A Climbing Instructor
on Denali*

Although the actual technical climbing on Denali is limited, many climbers forget that altitude, arctic conditions and heavy packs make thirty-five-degree snowslopes subjectively fifty-five degrees.

In the following accounts of fifteen falls on Denali, it is interesting to note that fourteen occurred during the descent and that all but one of those took place above fifteen thousand feet. The largest number of falls occurred on the descent traverse from Denali Pass to 17,200 feet on the West Buttress. One can surmise that the victims fell because they had altitude sickness or were worn out from the cold. Sickness, exhaustion or inexperience might make a climber stumble or preclude the use of good self-arrest technique; all could cause serious falls.

On June 2, 1972, a Ray Genet guided party reached Denali Pass but had to turn back because of high winds and poor visibility. A short way down, the "snow gave way" underneath Dick Witte's foot; he fell ten feet, until his crampon caught, and broke his left leg. He continued to fall down the thirty-degree slope for sixty feet until another client self-arrested and stopped the fall. Genet splinted Witte's leg and moved him down to the 17,200-foot camp, from which he was evacuated two days later by a gutsy helicopter pilot.

A year later, in 1973, another Genet guided party was descending below Denali Pass after their summit climb. One of the clients, Joe Wiley, was so affected by the altitude that he was unable to descend without a great deal of help. Some of the team members decided how they would make a faster descent: six members of the group began to slide down the slope in a self-arrest position. Greg Brown, the last person on the seven-man rope team, had not been told of this decision. After sliding fifty feet, the entire rope team lost control and slid four hundred to five hundred feet. Brown tumbled head over heels and suffered cuts, bruises and a concussion. That night, he was moved to 17,200 feet. The next day his condition improved and, with difficulty, he was helped to 14,200 feet where, together with another member of the team, Charles Schertz, who was uninjured, he was evacuated by an Army helicopter.

It is difficult enough for one person to perform a self-arrest. When an entire team, some of whose members are weary and sick, tries such a maneuver on a wind-packed, crevassed glacier, the results can be disastrous. Wiley should have been assisted down on the arms of the two strongest climbers.

The next fall at Denali Pass occurred in July 1976. A five-man Austrian traverse party was descending after having reached the summit. As Ortwin Wister was having trouble breathing, the leader, Helmut Linzbichler, sent Gunter Schmidt to catch up with a doctor in a Canadian party that was below them. At about 18,800 feet, Schmidt either slipped while peering over the edge or decided to descend directly to the Canadian party; he then fell 1,200 feet down the slope in front of the Canadians' traverse route and into a crevasse. He apparently died instantly from a broken neck. His body was never recovered. Like many other European climbers who approach the summit from the West Buttress, Schmidt carried ski poles rather than an ice ax for self-arresting.

Meanwhile, Wister, the climber with the breathing problem, recovered. Three of the Austrians went down the Muldrow Glacier route, while Linzbichler, who was unaware of Schmidt's death, descended the West Buttress to tell him that a doctor was not needed.

According to the Canadians, Schmidt had climbed to the summit quickly, had made jokes with them on top and was well acclimated. Linzbichler was evacuated by helicopter from 17,200 feet for a number of reasons: to prevent him from descending the Muldrow Glacier alone, to clarify problems with the Anchorage and Austrian press, and to notify Schmidt's next of kin.

Schmidt would have been able to self-arrest if he had carried an ice ax. Also, splitting a group up, which proved to be a mistake for the Austrians, should be avoided.

On May 11, 1980, another traverse party of four was ferrying loads to Denali Pass from 17,200 feet on the West Buttress. They were unroped but using crampons and ice axes. On the way back down, a German climber, Gerold Herrman, stumbled and took a tumbling fall. The other three took ten minutes to reach his body in a shallow crevasse. Although they performed CPR for thirty minutes, there was no response. They eventually lowered the body to 14,200 feet where it was evacuated on May 16, together with one member of the group.

At Denali Pass, altitude sickness or variable snow conditions can cause climbers to stumble. If this team had been roped together, Herrman's fall might have been stopped.

In 1982, two falls in the Denali Pass area resulted in evacuations. Both cases were classic examples of inexperienced, poorly led climbers getting in over their heads.

The first group was brought together through a University of Alaska mountaineering class. They named their expedition "Denali 101" and used a computer and a local guide as a consultant to plan their trip.

During their first week on the glacier, two members of the group abandoned the expedition because of personality conflicts. Two weeks later, the rest of the group split in two on their way to the summit. One member of the slower group had acute mountain sickness (he collapsed and was incoherent), so they immediately radioed the National Park Service and asked about the feasibility of a helicopter evacuation. They were advised to descend and call back in an hour with a progress report.

The sick climber improved as he descended to 17,200 feet but, because of a blind spot, the group could not radio back to the National Park Service. Fortunately, military helicopters, assuming the worst, mobilized in Talkeetna. Meanwhile, a woman in the second group slipped during the descent from Denali Pass. The other members of her rope team stopped her with an ice-ax arrest; however, she had broken her ankle. This information was radioed to a military plane that was flying around the mountain. The next day, after the woman was brought down to 17,200 feet, the helicopters responded immediately. Another member of the group realized he had gotten frostbite on his feet while loading the woman into the helicopter; he was eventually taken down the mountain by dog sled. Of the ten people who started up the mountain, two left early, one had debilitating altitude sickness and two were evacuated.

This group's high attrition rate could be attributed to their inexperience and lack of cohesiveness as a team. A group such as this should never consider splitting apart, thus weakening themselves further. Their first reaction to altitude sickness was to inquire about a helicopter rather than to descend immediately. Denali 101's origin in a college classroom was a contrived and unrecommended means of team selection. Ideally, an expedition should be composed of friends who have climbed together. Their initial plan to hire a guide, which was not carried out, might have given them the leadership they lacked.

Nine days later, on May 26, 1982, an eighteen-member Genet Expeditions guided party from the German Alpine Club left for the summit from 17,200 feet in deteriorating weather conditions. Two of the three guides remained behind because they were sick and also because of a disagreement about making a summit attempt in poor weather. At Denali Pass, visibility was twenty to thirty yards with high winds but the climbers continued. Below Kahiltna Horn, the head guide turned back with two clients but was roped into just one of them. On the way down from Denali Pass, the unroped client fell, dropped her ice ax and slid twelve hundred feet, sustaining several compression fractures of her vertebrae.

Meanwhile, the remainder of the party had turned around below the summit headwall because of the deteriorating weather conditions. One client collapsed and had to be supported all the way down. Below Denali Pass, the climbers were unroped and most of them used ski poles instead of ice axes. Three men slipped and fell in the freshly fallen snow but were unhurt. By accident, they met the head guide and the two clients but couldn't find their way back to the 17,200-foot camp because of whiteout conditions. They then spread out and bivouacked in the open. They had no shovels to dig in with, no stoves and no radio.

The next morning the weather was clear with 70–100 mph winds and the group made it back to 17,200 feet where they asked Ranger Roger Robinson for help. In addition to one client who suffered a back injury, all of the group were hypothermic and two people had frostbitten fingers. Because their tents had blown down, Robinson helped the group to find shelter in caves with other climbers. The next day, when the storm had abated, they descended to 14,200 feet, where three clients were evacuated in a military helicopter along with another client who had suffered frostbite in the same storm.

This group made numerous mistakes. The disagreement over the weather should have precluded a summit attempt that day. Also, going to the summit with only one out of three guides showed poor judgment. The head guide should have brought the entire group back down, instead of allowing them to split up and proceed without a guide. All of the clients should have been roped together; they should have carried ice axes, stoves, a radio and a shovel to dig in with. If the weather had been worse, this group would not have survived.

Many Germans who go to Denali underestimate both the mountain and its weather. Statistics show that from 1973–82 Germans were involved in more accidents than any other nationality. (See Appendix I for incident rate by nationality.) It is unfortunate that these poorly led groups continue to make the same mistakes, such as climbing unroped without ice axes in poor weather, and that, inevitably, they jeopardize other climbers and the pilots who must rescue them.

Falls that occur while climbers are ascending are rare. Usually, inexperienced climbers fall on thirty- to forty-degree snow and ice slopes when returning from the summit with altitude sickness, in a state of exhaustion or in poor weather conditions. Experienced climbers who fall on technically difficult ground are forced to deal with the accident on their own.

At 2 A.M., on May 22, 1979, Ken Currens took a 240-foot leader fall when the snow ledge he was standing on collapsed. An ice screw thirty feet above his belayer, Jack Tackle, held the fall. They were on a steep, sixty-degree to vertical variation of the South Buttress route, an unclimbed, isolated spur of the Ruth Glacier. Tackle lowered Currens to a bergschrund and rappelled down to him. Although his helmet probably prevented serious head injury, he fractured his left femur.

Tackle gave him a pain killer, lowered him to their ice cave and skied out five miles to the Mountain House for help. At 4:30 P.M., he contacted Cliff Hudson with his CB radio and flew out with Hudson to Talkeetna to organize a rescue. He returned to the Ruth Glacier at 7:45 P.M. with Mugs Stump and Jim Logan. Four hours later, they had climbed up to the cave; at 1 A.M., they began three-hundred-foot lowers, with Stump belaying and Logan and Tackle on the Thompson litter with Currens. At 4 A.M., they arrived at the glacier and splinted Currens' leg with two snow pickets. By 7:30 A.M., helicopter pilot Jim Okonek and Hudson had evacuated all four to Talkeetna.

Tackle and Currens were competent climbers doing a hard route. After the accident, they dealt with the situation

Ken Currens being loaded into a helicopter
after his evacuation from the Isis Face in 1979.

JACK TACKLE

using better judgment, leadership and resourcefulness than parties five times their size have displayed on the West Buttress. Tackle could have fallen into a crevasse while skiing down for help but he understood that risk. They did carry a radio and managed their rescue with grace under fire. Tackle came back two more times with just a single partner and finally completed the route in 1982.

Between 1970 and 1982, there were four serious falls from the West Rib. In April 1970, a four-man party made the second ascent of the West Rib. At thirteen thousand feet, during their descent, either Gerald Smith or John Luz slipped and pulled the other off. They fell two thousand feet down the initial couloir to their deaths. Apparently, they were not attached to their fixed line when they slipped.

In June 1972, three Japanese women fell down the West Rib while descending from the summit. They were found dead at the fifteen-thousand-foot level by Ray Genet. It's likely that the three women were tired from their summit climb and that one of them slipped and pulled the others off the thirty-five- to fifty-degree snowslopes between 17,800 and 19,400 feet. In 1979 and 1982, similar accidents occurred again in the same gully.

In May 1979, three Korean climbers left from fourteen thousand feet on the West Rib for the summit. (This was an unreasonably long day and the group carried no water.) Later, they radioed down that they had made the summit but that they were very tired. According to one of the climbers, Hun-Kyu Park, the snow slipped out from under him on the descent and he fell; he expected the other two to self-arrest and stop him but they didn't. (What Park neglected to mention after the accident was that none of the team wore crampons; this was a major mistake and the cause of the fall.) The three climbers slid approximately 2,500 feet down the gully, stopping at 15,500 feet.

Luckily, before the weather deteriorated, they were seen from 14,200 feet. Again, the tireless Denali guide, Ray Genet, together with another guide, Brian Okonek, went up to the fallen climbers. San-Don Ko was dead and Li-Kyo Lee had severe head injuries. After placing Lee in a snow cave, they lowered Park to 14,200 feet on the West Buttress. When Okonek and four others went back for Lee, he was dead.

Park was attended to by Dr. Bing at the 14,200-foot camp. Bing, who just happened to be there, kept Park's frozen feet packed in snow but thawed his hands since they were already thawing. Later the same day, Park was airlifted from 14,200 feet by a helicopter. He had a badly dislocated knee and later lost the tips of his toes and many of the joints on his left hand to frostbite. Medical attention at the 14,200-foot West Buttress camp would once again prove invaluable for climbers who fell from the West Rib; so would Brian Okonek.

In May and June 1982, Dr. Peter Hackett and Okonek were part of a team manning the High Latitude Research Project (HLRP) tent at 14,200 feet on the West Buttress. On June 4, Okonek noticed two dots in the same spot where the Koreans had been three years earlier. Okonek and Hackett reached the two climbers, Takashi Kanda and Mamoru Ida; with help from eleven other climbers, they sledded them down to the heated medical tent at 14,200 feet.

Kanda and Ida both had head injuries and were put on IV fluids and oxygen. Ida had frostbite on his hands, feet and penis. The weather remained bad until June 7 and the situation became critical because ground teams couldn't make it up to the camp in the heavy snows to replenish the dwindling IV fluids needed for the injured pair. Finally, during a quick break in the clouds, Kanda and Ida were evacuated by an Army helicopter. Without the HLRP group, the two comatose Japanese would have died.

Okonek thought Ida's frostbite had developed prior to the fall and that the pair had been forced to bivouac in a storm. They probably slipped at about eighteen thousand feet while descending from the summit: like five other dead climbers who preceded them, victims of altitude sickness or their inability to self-arrest on the thirty-five- to fifty-degree snow. Perhaps one more acclimatization day at the 16,500-foot camp on the West Rib and sharper self-arrest

BRIAN OKONEK

A comatose climber, Takashi Kanda,
being rescued from the West Rib in 1982.

skills could prevent this accident from happening to other climbers. Nine Japanese have died on the mountain; climbers familiar with the gully's accident history have named it the "Orient Express."

Another fall involving Japanese climbers occurred on the Cassin Ridge in May 1974 when five members of an eight-man team, who had reached the summit, were rappelling back down the route. In the Japanese Couloir (named for the second-ascent team's variation on Cassin's route), two climbers rappelled down their 8mm fixed line. When a third climber, Yoshikazu Okado, started down, the rope broke. He fell eight hundred feet and was killed.

Fixed line is now a part of a bygone era on Denali. Nevertheless, rope still festoons the Cassin like historical graffiti. In 1967, Bill Phillips fell seventy feet while rappelling on Cassin's old line, which broke. Mike Helms wrote of an incident that occurred on the Cassin in 1980. When he clipped into an old line, it broke and he fell over backwards; miraculously, however, he stopped himself in what he called the closest call he'd ever had in the mountains. Even new fixed rope must be regarded as suspect due to sharp crampons, rockfall and abrasive weather.

Now, for reasons of safety and ethics, most climbers prefer to rely solely on their own climbing ropes and to walk down the West Buttress instead of rappelling their route. In deciding whether or not to bring fixed rope, climbers must recognize their own limitations. Instead of placing fixed lines on a difficult route, consider doing an alpine-style ascent of an easier one. Too often, climbers develop an unnecessary dependence on equipment instead of relying on their own skill and good judgment. The Sourdoughs and Archdeacon Stuck never heard of fixed rope.

On July 13, 1973, after climbing the South Peak, a National Outdoor Leadership School (NOLS) group attempted the North Peak from 17,600 feet on the Harper Glacier. While waiting to use a fixed line at the top of a couloir, one student took off his pack, anchored it to his ice ax and climbed up to a ropemate to ask a favor. He slipped and, without his ax, couldn't self-arrest; he pulled the other three climbers eight hundred feet down the couloir. (The students were "not terribly proficient at self-arrest techniques" and the snow surface was not conducive to self-arrests.)

The two other rope teams saw forms at the bottom of the couloir and started down from the 18,600-foot plateau. A two-man team slipped and fell to the bottom of the couloir; John Morrell broke his wrist in this fall. When they reached the bottom, they found that David Ober had broken his femur and that Dwayne Stranahan had broken his lower leg in the initial fall. The student who caused the fall was uninjured; he had been the major personality problem of the trip, lacking in both consideration and judgment.

The two climbers with leg injuries were injected with Demerol and the next day were dragged down to fifteen thousand feet in lashed-together pack frames. All three of the injured climbers were evacuated by an Air Force helicopter.

One instructor felt that "they had had plenty" in climbing the South Peak and had opted out of an attempt on the North Peak because he felt the group was not up to it psychologically. He stated, "Perhaps, given the length of the expedition, the general level of experience, the weather (mediocre) and the superstitious fact that all had gone pretty well so far, perhaps it would have been a wise decision not to push our luck. . . ."

Three years later, on July 11, 1976, the six-man Juneau Denali Expedition reached eighteen thousand feet on the Pioneer Ridge. The two strongest members of the group, Steve Swenson and Bruce Blume, were well ahead of the other four. They ultimately climbed over the North Peak and descended to Denali Pass. At 5 P.M., Larry Fanning became ill. Joe Ebner radioed out for advice and the Park Service recommended descent. Fanning had acute mountain sickness.

The four climbers decided that the Sourdough Couloir was a better choice than the North Peak or descending by their fixed ropes on the Pioneer Ridge. After failing to catch up with Swenson and Blume, they began their descent on

July 12. The couloir was difficult, with six inches of snow over ice, so they fixed ropes to their ice axes. Fanning had broken front points on one crampon. Eight hundred feet down, an ice ax pulled out and they all fell one thousand feet down the couloir. Ebner and Richard Rose died during the fall. Bill Joiner was delirious and was suspended upside down in the ropes; Fanning had broken his left leg in three places. He tried repeatedly, but unsuccessfully, to right Joiner and then searched for a radio in Ebner's pack but couldn't find one. Fanning spent the night without a hat or gloves while Joiner remained hanging upside down in the ropes.

Seventeen hours after the fall, a Canadian expedition came by. They moved Joiner and then returned and brought Fanning down to their camp at fifteen thousand feet. The National Park Service radioed a NOLS group who moved the bodies down to the Canadian camp at fifteen thousand feet and helped to treat Joiner and Fanning.

On July 14, Joiner regained consciousness. However, because of poor communications and the lack of a flight surgeon, the helicopter didn't arrive until 3:45 A.M. on July 15.

Splitting a group up is the most common prelude to accidents on Denali. In the case of the Juneau expedition, Swenson and Blume, the strongest members of the group, would have been a considerable asset to the team during their difficult traverse. The four remaining climbers should have chosen to descend the familiar Pioneer Ridge rather than the unknown Sourdough Couloir. Although they were probably short on hardware, fixing ropes to ice axes is unreliable; ice screws, pickets, flukes or pitons would have been best.

The cost of an Army evacuation of Joiner, Fanning and the two bodies was $11,464.00. The Bicentennial year on Denali was an expensive one for the taxpayer: $82,142.36 was spent on rescue flights. In June of that year, a helicopter pilot, Buddy Woods, charged the National Park Service $8,640.87 for an unprecedented, but bold, evacuation of two women from the very top of North America.

On June 2, 1976, four members of the Denali Women's Expedition slipped and fell four hundred feet while descending from the summit on the South Buttress. Jennifer Williams and Paula Kregel suffered minor injuries from hitting their heads on the slope. Williams also hit her head on an ice ax and was unconscious for a short time; Kregel was dizzy and could not walk. Vera Komarkova and Joan Williams left the two at 19,600 feet, climbed over the summit and down to Denali Pass to report the accident.

Meanwhile, a hang glider jumped off the summit, crashed and rolled eight hundred feet down the South Face, which confused matters. Shortly afterwards, a military plane made three airdrops of rope and litters to be used in the two separate evacuations; the airdrops were never found. The hang glider returned to the summit unscathed.

Komarkova's efforts to get a ground team to her injured friends failed; it was too hard to climb over the summit and then carry someone back up and down again at altitude. Ray Genet and pilot Buddy Woods were both extremely anxious to try a helicopter rescue. Finally, when the National Park Service realized there was no other alternative, they gave Woods permission to attempt a rescue. Woods dropped Genet off at 20,100 feet, literally on the summit, and Genet descended to Williams and Kregel. He found that their injuries were not as serious as originally estimated by Komarkova. He assisted Williams down a short distance, where Woods boldly hovered on the edge of a crevasse, and loaded her into the helicopter. Genet and a climber who had been dropped off with him moved Kregel down to a plateau at 18,700 feet, northeast of the summit; Woods then picked up both Kregel and the other climber. After transferring Kregel to an airplane on the Kahiltna Glacier, Woods returned for Genet.

No helicopter had ever landed that high on Denali before. (In 1980, Mike Covington had evacuated a client with HAPE from the same spot because a helicopter rescue was not feasible.) Without Woods, Genet, the third rescuer and a bit of luck, the two climbers would have died.

The Bicentennial year attracted a record number of climbers who were involved in a disproportionately high number of rescues. Climbers knew that they could call for a helicopter if they were in trouble and that rescues were seldom, if ever, denied. It is more than likely that the availability of helicopters on Denali prompted both brash climbing attitudes and a lack of initiative in self-evacuation; both of these can be fatal in more isolated areas such as the Cordillera Blanca in Peru or the Himalaya.

The next year, 1977, a veteran climber fell and broke his ankle on a hard route on Mount Hunter, Denali's neighbor. The climber's two companions lowered him down four thousand feet of steep ice and helped him into an airplane at the landing strip. They never considered a helicopter winch evacuation, nor did they carry a radio. The two remaining climbers, Mike Kennedy and George Lowe, finished the new route on Mount Hunter and then climbed a new route on nearby Mount Foraker. They were accomplished climbers setting a stylish example that few injured parties on Denali chose to repeat. Many inexperienced climbers are drawn to Denali because of its reputation; once injured, however, they lack the skill to perform a self-evacuation.

There have been fourteen deaths on Denali as a result of climbing falls, which are the most common type of accident on the mountain; these falls almost always occur during the descent. Prevention of altitude sickness and exhaustion and avoidance of trying for the summit in mediocre weather could reduce the number of falls. Proper ice-ax training could help in arresting slides. When all preventive measures fail, climbers must learn how to evacuate themselves to a lower elevation.

SUMMARY: CLIMBING FALLS

DATE	NAME	ROUTE & ELEVATION OF INCIDENT	COMMENTS
4/29/70	LUZ SMITH	W RIB 13000	SLIPPED, NOT ATTACHED TO FIXED LINE
6/4/72	WITTE	W BUTTRESS 18000	SNOW GAVE WAY
6/29/72	SACHIKO TOYAMA YAJIMA	W RIB CA. 18000	FELL 1500-2500 FEET WHILE DESCENDING
5/29/73	BROWN	W BUTTRESS 17500	ALTITUDE SICKNESS, GROUP SELF-ARREST FAILED
7/13/73	OBER MORRELL STRANAHAN	HARPER GLACIER 18800	FELL 800 FEET
5/27/74	OKADO	CASSIN 12200	FIXED ROPE BROKE ON RAPPEL, FELL 800 FEET
6/2/76	WILLIAMS KREGEL	S BUTTRESS 19600	FELL 400 FEET
7/12/76	EBNER ROSE FANNING JOINER	PIONEER RIDGE 16900	PARTY SEPARATED, ICE AX ANCHOR FAILED
7/21/76	SCHMIDT	W BUTTRESS 18800	NO ICE AX, UNROPED, FELL 1000 FEET
5/22/79	CURRENS	S BUTTRESS 10000	240-FOOT LEADER FALL
5/29/79	KO LEE PARK	W RIB 18000	SLIP, SELF-ARREST FAILED
5/11/80	HERRMAN	W BUTTRESS 18000	UNROPED
5/16/82	MCDANIEL	W BUTTRESS 17500	ROPED FALL
5/26/82	FROHN	W BUTTRESS 18000	UNROPED, FELL 500 FEET
6/4/82	KANDA IDA	W RIB 18800	FELL 2000 FEET WHILE DESCENDING

HOW EVACUATED	RESULT	RESCUED BY	GOVERNMENT COST
BURIED ON MOUNTAIN	2 DEATHS		NONE
HELICOPTER	BROKEN LEG	*	$2000
AIRPLANE	3 DEATHS	SHELDON	$4000
HELICOPTER	CONCUSSION	*	$1000
HELICOPTER	BROKEN FEMUR BROKEN LEG BROKEN WRIST	AIR FORCE	$1200
HELICOPTER	DEATH	ANCHORAGE HELICOPTER SERVICE	$1250
HELICOPTER	MINOR INJURIES	WOODS AIR SERVICE	$8640.87
HELICOPTER	2 DEATHS	ARMY	$11464
LEFT ON MOUNTAIN	DEATH	*	$5644
HELICOPTER	BROKEN FEMUR	AKLAND HELICOP-TER SERVICE	$3268.07
HELICOPTER	2 DEATHS, FROSTBITE	ARMY	*
HELICOPTER	DEATH	AKLAND HELICOP-TER SERVICE	$3268.07
HELICOPTER	BROKEN ANKLE	ARMY	**
HELICOPTER	COMPRESSION FRACTURE: VERTEBRAE	ARMY	**
HELICOPTER	HEAD INJURIES, FROSTBITE	ARMY	**

*INDICATES INFORMATION NOT AVAILABLE
**IN 1982, THE ARMY BILLED THE NPS $67,000 FOR ALL RESCUE OPERATIONS.

107

6
CREVASSE FALLS

Getting Ken out was an epic struggle. He is lucky to be alive and but for his strength and toughness probably would not be.

Ian Wade

Poor glacier-travel technique, such as slack ropes or no rope at all, is the primary cause of severe crevasse accidents on Denali. Falls may also occur after lunch or rest stops when the lead climber is not belayed out of the rest area, breaks through a bridge and falls until the rope tightens. One fatality occurred when a short rope was taut between two climbers. Unroped glacier travel has resulted in at least four confirmed (and one probable) deaths.

In 1932, the obstinate, yet very experienced, Allen Carpé was snowshoeing down the Muldrow Glacier unroped. Both he and his companion, Theodore Koven, died after falling into a crevasse. From the evidence, it appears that Koven had gone back up the glacier on skis to try and rescue Carpé from a crevasse and that he eventually fell into it himself.

A National Park Service Patrol dragged Koven's body (they could not find Carpé's) down the Muldrow, tied to their sled with a climbing rope. One ropeless ranger, Grant Pearson, almost became the third fatality when he fell into a crevasse and had to be rescued. Fortunately his injuries were slight.

In February 1967, Jacques Batkin, an experienced French climber who had cut his teeth on the French Ridge of Mount Huntington a few years earlier, died in a crevasse fall a mile from Kahiltna base camp at seven thousand feet; he was unroped. Although another member of the team had fallen into the same crevasse the day before, the crevasse was left unwanded.

Apparently, Batkin was an irrepressible individual who preferred travelling alone. His fall could probably have been prevented if he had been aware of the earlier fall. Communication about dangers is important as there are many other strong, individualistic climbers like Batkin who solo Denali's glaciers.

In June 1971, four members of a National Outdoor Leadership School party arrived at a 9,300-foot campsite. They remained roped while they marked out a circle and probed for crevasses. Then, Dr. Bob Bullard took off his snowshoes, untied himself from the rope and took one step out of the probed circle. He broke through a crevasse bridge and grabbed the middle of a rope that was lying at his feet. He slid down the rope while Randy Cerf held one end and another member of the group dived unsuccessfully for the other. Although it appeared that Bullard was momentarily held by Cerf, the rope ultimately went slack as Bullard let go.

He fell one hundred thirty feet to his death at the bottom of the crevasse. Gary Ullin, an experienced climber with another party, rappelled down into the crevasse and tied a rope to the body. It was then hauled up and dragged down to 7,300 feet. On July 2, Don Sheldon flew the body out.

Bullard's reasons for stepping outside the probed area are not known. This accident shows the possibility of human error even when rest areas have been carefully probed.

In April 1976, during their approach to the Cassin Ridge, a six-man party stopped for a rest at 10,300 feet on the East Fork of the Kahiltna. Ian Wade and Ray Smutek started off; ten minutes later, Ken Jern followed in their tracks but was not belayed out of the rest area. After half a rope length, he broke through a crevasse bridge and fell seventy feet to the bottom, landing on his buttocks. Like many climbers leaving rest stops, he was not belayed; in part, this was because Wade and Smutek had passed over the same area without incident. The party had been worried about crevasses earlier in the day, while in an icefall, but had relaxed in the rest area because it was flat and they could not see any surface sinking that would indicate crevasses.

Wade rappelled down into the crevasse and dug Jern out from under some ice blocks which had fallen onto him. It took three hours to haul him out; he was unconscious and extremely hypothermic. The night of April 11, he was delirious.

They nursed Jern for the next three days. Eventually his condition began to improve and he was able to walk alone, but with difficulty. They had sent two climbers out to the landing strip but the radio was not there yet; they could not use their own CB radio because they were not up high enough. Finally, on April 17, a bush pilot was notified at the landing strip and Jern was evacuated the following day.

One means of reducing the severity of crevasse falls would be to consistently belay out of rest stops, regardless of the interpretation of the terrain. There are many good climbers who have overlooked similar small, but important, aspects of glacier-travel technique and paid dearly for their carelessness.

Two weeks after Jern was evacuated, a party on the Muldrow Glacier split up when one of their sleeping bags blew away at 10,700 feet; two of the climbers started down. At seven thousand feet, when Andrew Stepniewski was passing Carl Ellingsen, he broke through a crevasse bridge and fell sixty feet to the bottom. At the time, there was a great deal of slack in the rope.

Ellingsen got Stepniewski out with help from another party. He was unconscious for fifteen minutes, then became delirious. He suffered a minor concussion but was able to walk out several days later.

112

Ken Jern being assisted after
his crevasse extrication in 1976.

JONATHAN WATERMAN

John Thackray crossing a crevasse in
the Northeast Fork of Kahiltna Glacier.

Many people might describe this incident as a run of bad luck. Another interpretation is that the pair were actually very *lucky* to have made so many mistakes with only minor consequences. Equipment as invaluable as a sleeping bag should be tied down and slack in the rope negates the inherent advantages of roped travel. It was also very fortunate that another party was nearby to assist in removing Stepniewski from the crevasse.

On March 13, 1982, a British climber, Roger Mear, roped up with a Spaniard he did not know and started up the Kahiltna Glacier to retrieve a cache of gear. As Mike Young and I could not help because our feet were frostbitten, we remained in a snow cave at the seven-thousand-foot landing strip. Because of the language barrier, Mear and the Spaniard could not communicate with one another. The Spanish climber moved behind Mear, leaving a lot of slack in the rope. Possibly, he was unfamiliar with Denali's hidden crevasses and with proper glacier-travel techniques. Two miles out from base camp, Mear broke through a crevasse bridge and fell thirty feet to the bottom because of the slack in the rope. He severed some ligaments in his knee but was able to jumar out. The Spaniard left Mear to get help; meanwhile, Mear tied his skis together and pushed himself a mile down the glacier, where he met the three Spanish climbers who dragged him back to the landing strip on a sled. We all waited three more days for our overdue bush pilot to evacuate us from the landing strip.

Mear's accident illustrates the importance of having good communication and ropemates who have climbed together before.

In mid-April 1981, John Mallon Waterman set out alone up the Northwest Fork of the Ruth Glacier to solo a new route on the East Buttress. One party observed that his tracks made a beeline through a heavily crevassed area. Another party saw his snowshoe tracks and described them as a "crazy route in and out of slots [crevasses]." An old campsite was found at 7,200 feet on the glacier but, despite extensive air and ground searches, no further trace of Waterman was ever found. Waterman had soloed Mount

A body recovery from a crevasse.

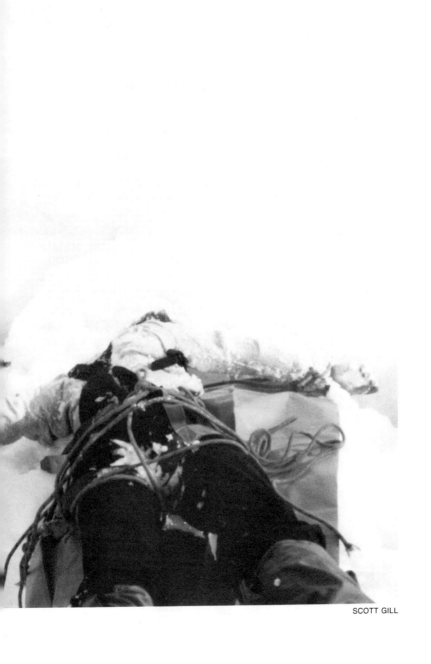

SCOTT GILL

Hunter in 1978; an incredible 145-day climb. Both Carpé and Batkin were very similar to Waterman, in that they had considerable experience on Alaskan peaks and were strong, individualistic climbers who felt comfortable on the mountain alone and unroped.

One could speculate that such personality traits, combined with a relaxation of attention to dangers, caused their crevasse deaths. Less experienced, team-oriented climbers who rope in have a better chance of surviving. It is also interesting to note that all three of these climbers wore snowshoes, which are not as safe in crevassed areas as skis.

On May 8, 1981, Jim Wickwire and Chris Kerrebrock, two strong, experienced climbers, were involved in a horrible accident on Denali. They were walking together on a short, twenty-foot rope, at 6,700 feet on the Peters Glacier, en route to the Wickersham Wall. They were both attached by nylon webbing to one large sled that was between them. Although Kerrebrock had previously fallen thigh deep into several crevasses, they had presented no real problem because the two were roped together. Just before the accident, they had come onto an area of glacier which seemed safe because they could not see any sagging snow bridges or crevasses (Jern's party had made the same observation). Suddenly Kerrebrock fell into a hidden crevasse and Wickwire was pulled through the air; he landed on top of both the sled and Kerrebrock, twenty-five feet down in a narrow crevasse.

Kerrebrock was wedged in very tightly and, despite hours of intense effort, Wickwire could not free him. First, he tried pulling Kerrebrock out from outside the crevasse; then he tried from the inside, by stepping into a sling-pulley. He also tried to chop Kerrebrock out and, in futility, attempted to cut Kerrebrock's pack off with an ice hammer. Wickwire finally gave up. As he had broken his shoulder in the initial fall, he was unable to use his arms anymore.

Kerrebrock died from hypothermia about three hours later. So that others could learn what had happened to them,

Kerrebrock had told Wickwire not to solo up the glacier and possibly meet a similar fate. Wickwire waited five days for a plane to fly over because he was in a walled-in area and their cb radio could only transmit line-of-sight. On the sixth day, he slowly picked his way up the Peters Glacier, probing each step of the way to locate other crevasses. He was finally picked up by glacier pilot Doug Geeting in a tricky landing near Kahiltna Pass.

Although using a short rope was convenient for dragging the sled and seemed safe initially, a longer rope would have had greater stretch and absorption and could have prevented Wickwire from being pulled into the crevasse on top of Kerrebrock. Also two sleds, instead of one heavy sled pulled between the climbers, might have proved a safer means of transport.

Careful attention to every detail of glacier travel is essential in order to prevent crevasse falls. Ropes should be sixty to one hundred feet long and should be kept taut or belayed between climbers. Even if a glacier seems safe, treating it casually has led to the deaths of several climbers. Crevasses must be probed for at every rest area. Jumar and crevasse rescue techniques must be practiced before starting up the glacier. Also, it is important to remember that the temperature inside a crevasse is below zero; many crevasse falls are compounded by hypothermia because the victim was scantily clad while travelling on the hot surface of the glacier.

Five climbers who enjoyed the sense of freedom and speed that soloing provides have been killed on Denali's glaciers. Unroped travel has become popular, particularly on the crowded Kahiltna Glacier. If this popularity continues, it is more than likely that other climbers will die inside a cold, dark hole before they begin to climb the mountain.

SUMMARY: CREVASSE FALLS

DATE	NAME	ROUTE & ELEVATION OF INCIDENT	COMMENTS
6/24/71	BULLARD	MULDROW 9300	UNROPED, STEPPED OUT OF PROBED AREA
4/11/76	JERN	E FORK KAHILTNA 7000	NOT BELAYED OUT OF REST AREA
4/19/81	WATERMAN	NW FORK RUTH 7200+	DISAPPEARED, PROBABLE CREVASSE FALL
5/1/76	STEPNIEWSKI	MULDROW 7000	PASSING WITH SLACK IN ROPE
5/8/81	KERREBROCK WICKWIRE	PETERS GLACIER 6700	SHORT ROPE
3/13/82	MEAR	W BUTTRESS 7000	LANGUAGE BARRIER, SLACK ROPE

HOW EVACUATED	RESULT	RESCUED BY	GOVERNMENT COST
SLED, AIRPLANE	DEATH	*	$300
HELICOPTER	2 CRUSHED VERTEBRAE, BROKEN ARM, MINOR FROSTBITE ON HAND	INTERNATIONAL AIR TAXI	$3453.07
BODY NEVER RECOVERED	DEATH	NPS	$6211.12
ON FOOT	MINOR CONCUSSION		NONE
HELICOPTER ON FOOT, PLANE	DEATH BROKEN SHOULDER	NPS	$5203.25
SLED	SEVERED LIGAMENTS		NONE

*INDICATES INFORMATION NOT AVAILABLE

7
AVALANCHES

When Big Bertha let loose
the first thing I realized was the
horrible nature of the sound.
It was an awesome event and one
that left me shaken, almost limp,
because the power was so evident.

Alan Danson
South Buttress, 1982

Four Canadian and American climbers disappeared in July 1980 during an attempt on the Cassin Ridge route. A year later, three Japanese climbers vanished while attempting the American Direct route on the South Face. Although no trace of any of the seven climbers was ever found, it is supposed that they were buried and killed in avalanches.

Although avalanches constitute only eight percent of the serious accidents on Denali, they are killers. As steeper, harder routes become more popular, objective dangers will increase and climbers will have to be more wary of avalanches.

Snow and ice avalanches—like storms, crevasses and rockfall—are an objective danger that can be made ninety percent safer by route selection and timing and ten percent safer by luck. Rod Newcomb, who experienced an avalanche on Denali, advises, "The rule of thumb in avalanche prediction is that there is no rule of thumb."

For the purpose of clarity, avalanches will be divided into two groups: slab and climax avalanches, which are caused after a snowfall by spontaneous or human triggers, and hanging glacier and serac avalanches, which are caused by the spontaneous release of unstable ice formations.

124

Slab and Climax Avalanches

Rod Newcomb, President of the American Avalanche Institute, describes his avalanche encounter:

In the spring of 1963 Peter Lev and I were on the first ascent of the East Buttress of Denali. Other members of the expedition were Al, Jed, Fred and Warren. The avalanche lore of the climbers was limited. Only two, Warren and I, had been on a major expedition to a big mountain before. All the climbers had some skiing experience, but no practice with avalanche forecasting and control. Our knowledge of stability evaluation came primarily from the 1961 edition of *The ABC of Avalanche Safety*. We had an expedition copy with us.

On May 1, Peter and I began the climbing on the route and climbed the first difficult section immediately above base camp. This section became known as the Bulge and, as Jed describes it, "The route is over a sixty-degree snow and sugar ice slope with occasional open and hidden crevasses." Pete and I fixed this section with 5/16-inch manila rope. Fred and Jed followed with loads to be cached and eventually carried higher to Camp 1.

My diary of May 1 does not mention anything about dangerous snow conditions, but I remember noting the harder snow underlain by loose granular snow. Peter's diary reads for May 1, "Up at 4 A.M.—fantastic colors and cold and clear. Rod, Jed, Fred and myself leave at 5 A.M. for the Buttress and the first difficult pitch. I get the difficult lead. It is very steep, rotten ice overlain by rotten snow, then a foot thick snow slab. I am uncertain and very slow. I take most of the morning for the 150-foot lead. At the top we fix manila line and bring loads up." Pete must have been impressed by the snow conditions to note them in his diary. It was a difficult pitch since it was hard to get firm footing after breaking through the slab into the loose snow beneath. Pete may have been worried about an avalanche.

After we climbed the Bulge, I dismissed any thought of an avalanche on that portion of the route. Jed and Fred followed us and we all descended that same afternoon.

The next day (May 2) continued to be clear. I was climbing alone attached only to the fixed rope and had climbed the Bulge and was waiting for Pete and Jed who were a few minutes behind me. Peter's diary reads, "Bright and clear—up at 3 A.M., off by 4 A.M. Warren and Al go ahead to recon. Pass the Bulge quickly. We find this pitch easy climbing compared to yesterday—it is hard surface—but as I reach the point of greatest convexity the slab

125

breaks—avalanche. The fixed line holds Jed and me as snow sweeps over us. High up dangerous warm slopes. Argument with Warren. High ice avalanche breaks off southeast spur and sweeps over base camp and Fred (who remained behind) is okay, but what a fright. Eight huge sympathetic avalanches started."

I did not hear nor could I see the avalanche from where I was waiting. After I thought they should have arrived at the top of the Bulge, I started to descend when they topped the Bulge and reported the avalanche. It was estimated to be two hundred feet long and three hundred feet across, with a two-foot fracture.

Several things deserve comment. First, before the avalanche on the Bulge, a total of seven ascents and four descents were made in a period of twenty-four hours. The party that triggered the avalanche was on the eighth and ninth ascents.

Secondly, the avalanche on the Bulge was only a few hours before the large avalanches that occurred around the rim of the southeast fork of the Ruth Glacier. It was very apparent that these were the first warm days of spring with air temperatures near freezing during the heat of the day.

Thirdly, it is interesting to note that Peter mentions an argument with Warren. The argument was about the stability of the snow on the route above the bulge. Warren was killed on the Matterhorn in a climbing accident. I have learned that when members of a party differ in their stability evaluation, it is wise to bow to the judgment of the most conservative member. Some members of the party may know more about snow and may have more experience but they may be overlooking something that someone else has spotted or feels. All too often, a backcountry traveler is on some ego trip and tries to cross a slope which, if he could clear his mind and reflect on the stability of the slope, he would back off.

In 1978, Joseph Carmichael and Al Fons Aaporta were climbing the lower West Rib couloir immediately after a three-day storm. At the top of the couloir, they were caught in an avalanche and carried 1,500 feet to the bottom. It would appear that they triggered the avalanche themselves as the slope was probably heavily loaded with snow after the storm.

Carmichael dug both himself and Aaporta out of the avalanche. He then put Aaporta, who had a compound ankle fracture and an injured thigh, into a sleeping bag. The next morning, he skied out of the heavily crevassed and avalanche-prone Northeast Fork of the Kahiltna with a broken and sprained ankle. After six miles, he met another party which signalled a passing plane to land. Carmichael was evacuated on the spot and Aaporta was picked up by a helicopter that afternoon.

In May 1981, Mike Covington had a close call within twenty-four hours after a snowstorm on the West Rib. A large, spontaneous powder avalanche ran down the couloir and would have swept him off his feet if he had not been attached to a fixed line.

In May 1982, a one-hundred-foot-wide, six-inch-deep avalanche broke off beneath the weight of a solo climber and swept down from 13,300 feet to the bottom of the forty- to fifty-degree lower West Rib couloir. One of four Swiss climbers in the couloir was swept seven hundred feet to the bottom but was uninjured.

The area above the West Rib couloir is a concave, snow deposition zone. The slope angle is ten to thirty-five degrees, which allows snow to accumulate rather than sliding off. If climbers could avoid this and other similar deposition zones on the mountain for at least twenty-four hours after a storm, the snow would settle and be a lot safer to travel on. Unfortunately, because of the surplus of bad weather on Denali, climbers are sometimes forced to travel as soon as the storm clears.

Recently, in the Alps, there have been numerous accidents in which climbers have knocked rocks, cornices, avalanches and even themselves onto parties below. As the traffic on Denali increases, one more objective danger will have to be added to the list: climbers above.

In June 1982, a storm-loaded slope broke off beneath Jonathan Chester, Ben Read and Anne Fletcher as they descended to the East Fork of the Kahiltna from the West Fork of the Ruth Glacier. The group had waited out a two-day storm that had dropped two to three feet of snow and was accompanied by high winds.

Chester had lived through a devastating avalanche in the

Himalaya and all of them were aware of the avalanche potential on the East Fork; however, lack of food dictated descent. They were skiing, roped, on a twenty-five degree slope with Read first, followed by Fletcher and Chester. Read made a kick turn that triggered a slab avalanche between Chester and Fletcher and carried all three of them down two hundred feet. Chester did a cartwheel and cut his second finger severely on his ice ax. They dug themselves out, stopped Chester's bleeding and bandaged his hand.

The avalanche was three hundred feet wide and eighteen inches deep and the runout was one thousand feet below the fracture line. The climbers continued down to the landing strip where Chester received medical care from the High Latitude Research Program.

Given their situation, at the top of a storm-loaded pass and with no food so that they could wait for the slopes to settle, there is nothing else they could have done.

In June 1981, in a similar accident, three climbers were descending from 16,200 feet on the West Buttress because one member of the group was sick. Six feet of a new powder snow had fallen in the previous two days. Just below the fixed lines, the slope in front of the lead climber avalanched and all three were pulled down for six hundred feet. They were half buried in the light snow and were able to dig themselves out. Juan Hoyos' ax had cut his face and punctured his groin. At 14,200 feet, an Army doctor closed Hoyos' facial wound with fifteen stitches and he walked down to the landing strip.

Although it's obvious that travelling after a storm can be unsafe on freshly loaded slopes of twenty to thirty-five degrees, climbers like Hoyos have no choice if they're sick, out of food or must move while the weather permits. Nevertheless, there are places that can be avoided during unstable weather conditions. More than once, groups have camped at 14,400 feet on the West Buttress (directly under the slope leading to the fixed line) and have had their tents buried when the slope above avalanched spontaneously. Tents should be pitched as far from the fixed line basin as possible.

128

In June 1982, the Valley Mountaineers and the North Cascades Alpine School (NCAS) set up camp at 12,500 feet on the West Buttress route. Meanwhile, the Fantasy Ridge and Mountain Trip guided groups cached some gear nearby. That night, wet snow fell at the rate of one inch per hour and the winds were out of the southeast at twenty-five miles per hour. This was an unusual situation. The forty- to sixty-degree slopes were being loaded with wet snow that didn't slide off and continued to collect until morning. Very early in the morning, the two groups camped at 12,500 feet heard avalanches coming down the gullies from the West Buttress. At 6:30 A.M., an avalanche from a large bowl on the slopes above was funnelled down a gully towards their four tents and buried them under two to four feet of wet snow. The members of the Valley Mountaineers group were thrown out of their tents and one of them was buried for twenty minutes. As they lost their shovels in the avalanche, the NCAS group dug the climber out. Although two tents were destroyed, no one was injured. The NCAS group continued up the mountain, while the Valley Mountaineers retreated. The Mountain Trip group found their cache and continued their climb but, despite extensive digging and probing, the Fantasy group couldn't find theirs and two of the members retreated. (In 1978, an avalanche hit the Courtney–Skinner group at this site.)

In addition to avalanche potential, this area has extreme winds. Both of these hazards can be minimized, if not eliminated, by camping at the bergschrund at 12,900 feet.

Hanging Glacier and Serac Avalanches

The most dangerous avalanche zone on the entire mountain is the Wickersham Wall. After the first ascent, Hans Gmoser remarked that his group could not have survived a large snowstorm on the upper part of the route. Along with many dangerous low-angled snow deposition zones, the face is pockmarked with unpredictable hanging glaciers and seracs.

The Northeast Fork of the Kahiltna Glacier also rates high in objective dangers. Aside from crevasses, the valley is fringed with hanging glaciers and seracs. As it is a relatively narrow valley, many climbers have watched avalanches roar across the breadth of the glacier. Only two tent sites on the approaches to the West Rib and the Cassin can be considered marginally safe. One is on the top of a small hill, just before the icefall, which curves up around the West Rib. The second, above the icefall at 11,600 feet, hugs the eastern side of the valley in order to avoid the potential slide path of a hanging glacier on the Southwest Face.

In July 1980, the Toronto Cassin Expedition started up the Northeast Fork of the Kahiltna. They carred a CB radio but, despite three hundred man hours of aerial searching, were never heard from or seen again. As of winter 1982–83, their four bodies had not been found: the area has become known as the "Valley of Death."

Mike Helms wrote about the avalanche that he experienced while camping at about nine thousand feet on the Northeast Fork in June 1980:

June 5 started out as a lovely day. We were all four up early, enjoying the morning sunshine as an opportunity to dry our bags and to warm ourselves. I was savoring my second or third cup of coffee when I heard a loud crack from the icefall on the Kahiltna Peaks immediately behind us. I looked to my right and saw Bob running across the glacier. I glanced back to my left and it seemed the whole side of the Kahiltna Peaks were in motion. That's when I started running. Simon [McCartney] and Jack [Roberts] were still in their tent. Looking back over my shoulder I couldn't see our tents. They were totally obscured by a wall of snow. I do remember covering my face to make an air pocket and saying to myself, "Oh! Christ, not now, not like this." As the snow began to clear, I saw Bob walking back to camp. Both of us were white with snowdust. We were getting a good laugh out of our sprint when we walked into camp. What we saw when the dust cleared sobered us up immediately.

The avalanche had stopped a short six feet from our tents. It was the largest ice avalanche I had ever seen. Maybe a mile in width by a half mile; some of the blocks were as large as pickup trucks. The spot where Bob had originally stopped was buried under six to eight feet of cement-hard rubble! Jack's sleeping bag was drying in one of the tents. The air blast from the avalanche blew it nearly a quarter of a mile out onto the glacier.

Because of trail-breaking difficulties and tedious route-finding through the crevasses or whiteouts, many climbers, like Helms, often camp beneath hanging glaciers, not realizing that they are in a danger zone. In 1981, because of a whiteout, I camped at the same site as Helms. The next morning when it cleared, I was horrified to see that we were in the runout path of a hanging glacier. If we had camped another mile up the glacier, we would have been safe.

Some parties follow the original Cassin approach up the longer East Fork of the Kahiltna to avoid the more dangerous Valley of Death approach. Although the East Fork is wider and safer, it is still hazardous. In July 1982, a Norwegian party observed a tremendous serac avalanche sweep down from Peak 12,240, across the glacier, to within yards of their camp on the west side of the East Fork of the Kahiltna.

The preeminent, nightmarish hanging glacier on Denali is to be found at the upper end of the East Fork. It is perched at sixteen thousand feet on the South Face and is three quarters of a mile wide and three hundred feet high. It has been dubbed "Big Bertha" like its relative on the Khumbu Icefall on Mount Everest which was named after the Nazi artillery cannon.

During Mark Hesse's solo ascent of the South Face, Big Bertha released five minutes after he reached the bergschrund, just beyond the path of the airborne avalanche. (See photograph, pages 132-33.)

Climbers on the nearby South Buttress should tread with caution on the ramp between 12,000 and 15,500 feet where a hanging glacier and seracs threaten the entire route. The ramp is also quite dangerous after snowstorms. Tentsites should be chosen with care.

Big Bertha releasing in a continuous
4000-foot wave down the South Face.

MICHAEL COVINGTON

In July 1967, the South Buttress team supporting the American Direct South Face party had just descended the ramp from twelve thousand feet onto the East Fork. A serac at fifteen thousand feet on the ramp collapsed and the debris from the avalanche buried two members of the team up to their waists. The other two were blown forty yards into a crevasse.

In July 1981, a probable avalanche buried a Japanese team in the East Fork. Makoto Kinoshita, Masuaki Ohnishi and Osamu Ozaki had planned to climb the American Direct route. As they had already climbed the West Buttress in June, they were well acclimatized and knew what to expect on the mountain.

They were last seen at 9,200 feet on the East Fork by Mike Covington who was dragging out a frostbitten client. At that time, "the walls were coming down all over the glacier." Sometimes they had to stop talking because the roaring was so loud. Covington told the Japanese that his group "barely got away with their lives" and that "it was suicide to go up there" after such a big snowstorm. They said they would "go have a look" anyway. Another storm system moved in and two weeks later, after it cleared, the National Park Service began search flights for the Japanese team.

Covington felt that they never made it to the climb and that they were hit by an avalanche on the glacier. The only trace of the group was a tent they had left pitched on the Kahiltna Glacier. It is likely that the Japanese continued because of peer pressure. As Covington had warned them, they knew the route was dangerous but probably wanted to prove they could do it despite the odds against them.

In all potential avalanche situations, a conservative attitude, common sense and prior avalanche training are invaluable. Heavy snowfall, with or without wind, turns many slopes into deathtraps for at least twenty-four hours after a storm has abated. Wide variations in temperature, in the morning or evening, can also cause unstable conditions. If possible, routes underneath hanging glaciers should be avoided or sprinted through. Although few climbers on Denali carry avalanche beacons, they could help to save lives. Ski pole probes and large snow shovels are essential for digging out avalanche victims.

The American Avalanche Institute's President, Rod Newcomb, advocates a conservative, intuitive approach to potential avalanche zones. Avalanche expert Peter Lev has designed an *Avalimeter* which takes into account the safest periods of the year according to the tides. However, regardless of the precautions taken, luck still determines the outcome on some routes. The fact that seven climbers have been completely buried, without a trace, illustrates how large avalanches can be and how minuscule climbers are in comparison. Denali avalanches are deadly.

SUMMARY: AVALANCHES

DATE	NAME	ROUTE & ELEVATION OF INCIDENT	COMMENTS
5/29/78	CARMICHAEL AAPORTA	W RIB 12500	WITHIN 24 HOURS AFTER SNOWFALL
1978	COURTNEY SKINNER	W BUTTRESS 12500	DANGEROUS CAMP
6/5/80	HELMS	NE FORK 9000	DANGEROUS CAMP
7/80	CARROLL CHASE MANSON LEWIS	NE FORK OR CASSIN *	DANGEROUS GLACIER
5/81	COVINGTON	W RIB 12000	WITHIN 24 HOURS AFTER SNOWFALL
6/19/81	HOYOS	W BUTTRESS 15000	WITHIN 24 HOURS AFTER SNOWFALL
7/81	KINOSHITA OHNISHI OZAKI	E FORK OR AMERICAN DIRECT *	WITHIN 24 HOURS AFTER LARGE SNOWFALL
5/18/82	*	W RIB 12000	SWEPT OFF BY PARTY ABOVE
6/6/82	CHESTER READ FLETCHER	S BUTTRESS 12000	WITHIN 24 HOURS AFTER SNOWFALL
6/18/82	VALLEY MTNRS., N CASCADES ALPINE	W BUTTRESS 12500	DANGEROUS CAMP

HOW EVACUATED	RESULT	RESCUED BY	GOVERNMENT COST
AIRPLANE, HELICOPTER	2 BROKEN ANKLES	NPS	$4450
*	*		NONE
	UNHURT		NONE
BODIES NEVER RECOVERED	4 DEATHS	AIR FORCE, TALKEETNA AIR, AKLAND, ERA	$13987.62
	UNHURT		NONE
ON FOOT	ICE AX WOUND, 15 STITCHES		NONE
BODIES NEVER RECOVERED	3 DEATHS	*	$2575.65
	UNHURT		NONE
ON FOOT	WOUND FROM ICE AX		NONE
	UNHURT		NONE

* INDICATES INFORMATION NOT AVAILABLE

8
PRIOR HEALTH PROBLEMS AND EXHAUSTION

Great adventures are possible on Mount McKinley....providing those who attempt the mountains have served their long climbing apprenticeships first.

Doug Scott in
Alaska *Magazine, May 1977*

Unstable mental histories, abscessed teeth, diabetes, knee problems and general physical unpreparedness are examples of problems that can flare up out of all proportion on Denali. Any small medical problem can develop into a liability when it is combined with exposure to the cold, altitude and stressful living conditions on the mountain.

Prior Health Problems

On May 22, 1981, Steve Gall and I were guiding a seven-member party for Fantasy Ridge Expeditions on the West Buttress route. One of the clients, Ernest Chandler (49), could not travel without taking a rest every five or ten minutes because he was unfit and overweight. Although Gall took his drag sled and most of the weight from his pack, Chandler continued to take frequent rest stops. Towards the end of the day, after going up a hill at 7,600 feet, Chandler collapsed with a pain in his chest and was barely able to breathe.

As his wife, Evelyn, had panicked, I separated her from her husband. Then I calmed Chandler down, asked him to breathe slowly and relax, and put him in his sleeping bag. His pulse was high (92 per minute). There was pain in his chest when he took a deep breath and he had a headache. It also appeared that he might have a more serious problem, such as a pulmonary embolism or a heart condition. He confided to me that he had high blood pressure and had neglected to take his medicine that day.

That night, I slept next to Chandler and monitored his vital signs. I gave him warm drinks and a Valium capsule to help him relax. His pulse dropped to a normal sixty-eight. In the morning, he insisted that he should continue up the mountain. I decreed that he should neither continue nor walk back down to the landing strip, as I felt that he might collapse again and was unwilling to take the responsibility for a client on the glacier who was overweight and had high blood pressure. Gall and I arranged to have him flown out and Doug Geeting was able to taxi his plane right up to our tent, on a flat stretch of glacier at 7,600 feet.

Although I had asked for medical information on all of the clients prior to the trip, it was not available. Many guide companies have no real way of screening their clients until they arrive on the mountain. After Chandler flew off the mountain, he saw a doctor who diagnosed exhaustion; later that year, he was operated on for a ventral hernia. He came back the following summer and caused a considerable problem because he couldn't carry his share of the weight. He made it to 14,200 feet but was regarded as a liability. Physically unfit climbers on Denali have little chance of success.

In June 1982, a client in Michael Covington's Fantasy Ridge expedition, who had an unstable mental history, began talking about jumping off Kahiltna Pass and killing herself. Steve Gall accompanied her down to base camp where she became psychotic. At one point, she had to be restrained and was eventually sedated with Valium. Doug Geeting made a risky pickup in poor weather and flew her to the hospital. Her history of psychosis should have disqualified her from the trip.

Clients should be carefully screened by their guides and

This climber collapsed and died at 19,300 feet;
the body is one of 23 that remain on the mountain.

MIKE GRABER

present a full, accurate picture of the state of their health. Hopefully, guides on Denali will not have to deal with such prior health problems in the future.

On April 24, 1976, Jon Kushner, a diabetic, froze his two types of insulin at 14,200 feet on the West Buttress. After a radio miscommunication about the severity of his condition, he was evacuated by airplane from ten thousand feet on April 28 as he was descending to base camp. Although, apparently, Kushner could have made it down by himself, another party radioed (as often happens) that he needed an airlift.

He should, however, have taken better precautions against having his insulin freeze. The potential for insulin's freezing should be sufficiently obvious that any diabetic would insulate it inside a shirt or a sleeping bag.

In early July 1976, Gerhard Biederman was separated from his insulin at ten thousand feet by a three-day storm. When the group returned to camp after the storm, Biederman was in good shape but was given too much insulin and went into insulin shock. Jim Sharp made an emergency landing and evacuated him to the Providence Hospital in Anchorage.

As climbers are frequently pinned down by storms on Denali, Biederman should have taken this into account and carried his insulin at all times.

In July 1974, the leader of a four-man group was not able to descend below fifteen thousand feet on the Harper Glacier. He was picked up by a helicopter and, at the hospital, his problem was diagnosed as a septic-arthritic condition of the knee. It is not known whether he had a prior history of knee problems, but the importance of good knees is critical on Denali because heavy packs can turn clients with prior knee problems into basket cases.

Another problem that should be mentioned is dental health. In July 1973, a client of Ray Genet's was evacuated from 14,200 feet with an abscessed tooth. At least a handful of climbers have come to grief on Denali because of dental problems. As minor toothaches can develop into major ones at high altitude, dental checkups are a necessity before climbing Denali. The evacuation could have been prevented if the client had gone to a dentist prior to joining the expedition.

There have been many climbers on Denali who reduced their margin for success and caused other climbers and pilots to risk their lives for them by arriving on the mountain with small medical problems. Although, initially, these did not seem worth bothering about, they became more serious as the climbers went higher and stressful conditions whittled away at their reserves. It is essential for a climber to be in good health before attempting the mountain.

Exhaustion

On May 15, 1980, two Germans, Manfred Loibl and Margret Huschke, arrived in Talkeetna. The couple were on holiday in Alaska and had not initially planned to climb Denali. This lack of planning may have contributed to their poor state of preparedness and their eventual deaths. Few people, if any, have climbed Denali on impulse and these two underestimated the seriousness of the undertaking. They rented vapor barrier boots and crampons and borrowed snowshoes. Pilots Doug Geeting and Sonny Kragness were both concerned about their insufficient equipment. When Kragness asked if they had contacted the National Park Service Rangers, they replied that "their papers were in order." Because the two were from out of town and were probably not familiar with the regulations, they had not registered with the rangers. It is also unlikely that they had very much information about the mountain. They were flown in that day.

Reports from the mountain indicated that Loibl was very strong and that Huschke could barely keep up with him. On May 25, they made it to 17,200 feet and went to the summit two days later.

Another German climber, who met them at 19,500 feet, reported that they were exhausted and had asked him for food. Later, a guided party of Germans who met them just

Two climbers at 16,800
feet on the West Buttress.

JONATHAN WATERMAN

below the summit at 4:30 P.M. noted that the two were extremely exhausted. The weather was deteriorating and, at 5 P.M., when the group started down, they asked Loibl and Huschke if they would like to rope up with them. They declined, however, saying that they preferred to rest a little longer.

The two did not return to 17,200 feet that night and the weather became very bad, with high winds. Another climber, Mike McComb, who had a miserable bivouac at nineteen thousand feet on the West Buttress the same night, did not see the couple. Two days later, when the weather cleared, Ranger Dave Buchanan spotted Loibl's and Huschke's lifeless forms at 19,300 feet from an airplane.

On July 2, when guide Brian Okonek placed their bodies in a crevasse, he noticed that Loibl had a bruise on his forehead. It is likely that the exhausted couple sat down in the storm and died from hypothermia. Although they did carry a shovel to dig in with, they carried no food for their summit attempt, which probably contributed to their exhaustion. It would be a fair guess to say that Loibl and Huschke grossly underestimated the mountain and overestimated their own abilities. A Denali climb takes a tremendous amount of physical and mental preparation: an impulsive ascent is foolhardy.

In 1976, two climbers nearly met a similar fate. In their preclimb correspondence with the National Park Service, the leader wrote, "One of our members wants to be dumped in a crevasse (if he dies, that is) and for us to go on. What's the legality of this?" This was an unusual and, in light of what was to happen, prophetic letter. Such a casual attitude toward dying could well be the cause of many accidents on Denali.

On May 10, at 4:30 A.M., four members of the expedition started for the summit from 17,200 feet on the West Buttress. They reached Denali Pass at 10:30 A.M. and continued up to 19,500 feet, arriving there at around 5 P.M. Their water bottles had frozen at Denali Pass and two of the climbers were tired and decided to descend. The other two continued to the summit and bivouacked within two hundred feet of the top. As they had lost both bivouac sacks, they spent a very cold night; they also could not operate their stove.

By morning, one of them had severely frozen hands. They descended, taking a bad fall, and spent a second night out at 19,500 feet. They were discovered by Dougal Haston and Doug Scott who were descending the West Buttress after a grueling climb of the South Face and an uncomfortable bivouac on the summit. They were too exhausted to help the pair but descended to 17,200 feet and notified the rest of their party. (It is interesting to note that an overwhelming majority of climbers who bivouac near the summit bring themselves to the point of exhaustion. This can lead to hypothermia, frostbite and, sometimes, death. The combination of cold and altitude should preclude bivouacs above eighteen thousand feet.)

Fortunately, two other members of the party were able to assist the pair down that day. All four of the climbers who were involved in the summit attempt were flown out from 14,200 feet the next day. The two who spent two nights out above nineteen thousand feet lost extensive portions of their hands and feet. One had worn tight-fitting neoprene socks which probably contributed to the severity of his frostbite.

It had taken them six hours to go from 17,200 feet to Denali Pass, a trip that normally takes three hours at the most. At that point, they should have turned back. Their frozen water bottles could have been insulated under their shirts; this would have helped to prevent dehydration and, in turn, exhaustion and frostbite. Their subsequent altitude sickness affected their judgment and it was only luck that prevented them from being buried in a crevasse, as they had inquired about in their preclimb letter.

SUMMARY: PRIOR HEALTH PROBLEMS AND EXHAUSTION

DATE	NAME	ROUTE & ELEVATION OF INCIDENT	COMMENTS
7/31/73	BAKER	W BUTTRESS 14200	ABSCESSED TOOTH, NO PRIOR DENTAL CHECKUP
7/31/74	LEWITT	HARPER 15000	SEPTIC-ARTHRITIC KNEE, PRIOR HISTORY
4/28/76	KUSHNER	W BUTTRESS 14200	DIABETIC SHOCK, INSULIN FROZE
5/10/76	THOMPSON WILLIS	W BUTTRESS 20000	DEHYDRATION, EXHAUSTION, 2 HIGH BIVOUACS
7/5/76	BIEDERMAN	W BUTTRESS 10000	INSULIN SHOCK, SEPARATED FROM INSULIN, OVERDOSE
5/27/80	LOIBL HUSCHKE	W BUTTRESS 19500	ILL-PREPARED, EXHAUSTION, HYPOTHERMIA
5/22/81	CHANDLER	W BUTTRESS 7600	OVERWEIGHT, HIGH BLOOD PRESSURE, COLLAPSE
6/13/82	FANTASY RIDGE CLIENT	W BUTTRESS 10000	PSYCHOSIS

HOW EVACUATED	RESULT	RESCUED BY	GOVERNMENT COST
HELICOPTER	RECOVERED	ARMY	$1000
HELICOPTER	*	NPS	$2000
HELICOPTER	*	ARMY	$3912
HELICOPTER	FROSTBITE, EXTENSIVE AMPUTATION	ARMY	$3249
AIRPLANE	*	JIM SHARP	NONE
BURIED ON MOUNTAIN	2 DEATHS	TALKEETNA AIR TAXI	$303
AIRPLANE	VENTRAL HERNIA OPERATION	TALKEETNA AIR TAXI	NONE
ON FOOT	*	TALKEETNA AIR TAXI	NONE

* INDICATES INFORMATION NOT AVAILABLE

9
HOW TO PREPARE FOR DENALI

Not a single mishap had occurred to mar the complete success of our undertaking—not an injury of anyone, nor an illness.

Hudson Stuck in
The Ascent of Denali

Even though this chapter does not discuss a specific category of accident as do the preceding chapters, careful preparation for an expedition to Denali can in itself be a major factor in preventing many types of accidents.

In 1967, Boyd N. Everett, Jr. wrote *Organization of an Alaskan Expedition.* Although it was never formally published, this widely read report has been highly respected over the years as the best source of information on preparing an expedition to the Alaskan peaks. This chapter is based upon that timeless report and some of the information is taken directly from Everett's material.

Sources, services and references pertaining to the topics in this chapter are listed in the appendices. Appendix referrals are noted in the text.

TEAM

Choosing a Team

Boyd N. Everett, Jr. wrote that probably the most important factor in choosing a party for an expedition is that each man be congenial and able to live with every other man under strenuous conditions for a period of weeks. Social compatibility is essential. Almost never will it pay to take the exceptionally strong but humorless and unresponsive technician over a congenial but less technically oriented man. For most routes, it is probably best to have a party of similar technical ability and physical strength. Having climbers of about the same age may be desirable, particularly if the group is young. On potentially difficult routes, it might be desirable to have a few men of exceptional ability for the difficult leading.

Experience

Each climber should be seasoned in winter mountaineering, have experience in first aid and a thorough understanding of crevasse rescue. Everyone should be familiar with altitude-related problems and more than one person in the group should have some avalanche schooling. Prior cardiovascular training, such as running, biking, ski-racing, swimming or hiking with a heavy pack, can improve one's performance on the mountain. Good campcraft (snow caving, cooking and backpacking skills) is an essential part of a Denali trip, perhaps even more so than technical climbing ability.

Party Size

The optimal team size is four members, although experienced, expeditionary mountaineers often climb in two-man teams. A party of three or four has greater strength in terms of lead climbing, trail breaking and self-rescue capabilities. The larger the party, the more safely and slowly it will move.

Leadership

Every party has its own conception of leadership. Two-man teams have the fewest problems with respect to leadership decisions, while large expeditions can spend an entire day negotiating. Although some parties act democratically, many groups (usually foreign) elect one member who is more experienced and respected than the rest to be the leader. The leader's responsibility must be agreed upon before the team gets to the mountain. The best leaders are good followers and only make themselves heard when the situation demands it. Guided expeditions, however, have been observed to work well under somewhat authoritative guide-leaders who would be considered abrasive under any other circumstances.

Guides

Many individuals choose to hire a guide because of their lack of familiarity with the mountain, time constraints that prevent them from planning the trip properly, or their inexperience.

Denali National Park and Preserve has issued six concessionaire guide permits and one educational use permit. These guide services are listed in Appendix J.

Solo Climbs

Although five routes on Denali have been done solo, most of the climbers involved made arrangements to travel roped to others on crevassed glacier approaches. For the vast majority of Denali aspirants, soloing would be suicidal for obvious reasons. One of the most experienced climbers in the Alaska Range was killed in a solo attempt in 1981.

ROUTE PLANNING

Information and Resources

There is a great deal of information available on Denali routes. *The American Alpine Journal* publishes route descriptions and photographs almost every year. Excellent black and white photographs and a map are available from the Museum of Science in Boston. *The Canadian Alpine Journal, Climbing, Mountain* and *The Mountain World* all have fine photographs of and articles about Denali. (See Appendix K.)

Route ratings

Fifteen routes have been rated as easy to moderate, moderate, hard, difficult, and very difficult. The route names and ratings are listed in Appendix L.

Route recommendations

Denali is attempted by over six hundred fifty climbers per year. More than four hundred of them choose the West Buttress, while the West Rib, the Muldrow and the Cassin Ridge are next in order of popularity. Beginning expeditionary mountaineers should consider the Muldrow or West Buttress routes. The 1954 South Buttress or the Pioneer Ridge would be fine choices for mountaineers with expeditionary and cold weather experience who are looking for isolated, nontechnical routes. Experienced, expeditionary climbers have a wide range of routes to choose from. The South and East Buttresses harbor many difficult variations with no traffic to contend with. If fixed ropes are being considered, it is recommended that an easier route be chosen instead.

Route Times

Whereas climbers often overestimate the pure technical difficulty of a route, there is a definite tendency to underestimate how many days it will take to climb a given route. Climbers accustomed to looking at two thousand- and three thousand-foot walls in the Canadian Rockies will have difficulty gauging distances when they look at photographs of Alaska's eight thousand- to ten thousand-foot (and higher) vertical rises. Even when the mountains are properly evaluated for size, climbers overestimate their ability to move in them. There are several reasons for this. For many climbers, there are initial psychological barriers that prevent them from working efficiently. Uncertainty about climbing and avalanche conditions is also a factor. Low-altitude climbing done at night will require more time than if done during the day. On the bigger mountains, altitude will slow the party somewhat, particularly while backpacking. There is a tendency to underestimate the time required for camp chores. Meals usually require two hours or more to prepare. Breaking camp, including a meal, takes three to four hours. It shouldn't take this long but it does. Six hours for eating and camp chores per day plus eight hours for sleeping leaves only ten hours per day, sometimes less, for actual climbing. This compares with twelve to fourteen hours for most other mountains. Weather factors will often shorten many climbing days as well as decreasing the efficiency of the climbers.

Climbers leaving from the Southeast Fork of the Kahiltna should leave behind six days of food in case they're stormed in while waiting for a flight out. Even with bad weather, the climb should not take more than three and one half weeks from the landing strip. Under ideal conditions, parties have climbed the mountain in two weeks, although this is exceptionally fast. Trying to climb Denali in less than two weeks would not allow for adequate acclimatization. Many beginning parties take more than four weeks because of superfluous supplies, excessive load ferrying and ponderous climbing styles.

DENALI NATIONAL PARK AND PRESERVE

Requirements

In recent years, the National Park Service has loosened the old climbing requirements (radios, permission to climb, party size and experience levels) because they were ineffective and impossible to enforce. Now, the Park Service works mainly in advising climbers as well as coordinating rescues and cleaning up trash on the mountain. With the exception of some Fairbanks climbers, the majority of climbers have found that the requirements are quite simple and that they do not interfere with their climbing experience.

There are two requirements for expeditions planning climbs in Denali National Park and Preserve: 1. Expeditions to Denali and Mount Foraker must submit individual registrations to the mountaineering rangers prior to departure. (To avoid confusion, it is imperative that one team member handle all correspondence with the National Park Service, air carriers and support organizations. The name of the expedition should be used on all correspondence.) 2. Climbers should check in with the National Park Service Mountaineering Rangers in Talkeetna or at Denali Park Headquarters before and after the climb.

Rangers

The Talkeetna Ranger Station is manned by the rangers from early April until late August. The Ranger Station is also a climbers' resource library with books, photographs, magazine articles and maps of the Alaska Range. The rangers are hired for their expertise on Denali, their rapport with climbers and their emergency medical and rescue backgrounds. They keep their fingers on the pulse of all Alaska Range activities by meeting all of the climbers, monitoring a CB radio in Talkeetna and performing regular climbing and cleanup patrols on the mountain.

RESCUE

Brian Okonek, a Denali climber and guide, wrote: "Far too many parties are crying wolf. This is a scary reality. A few false rescues and climbers, pilots and the National Park Service will begin to think that all rescue calls are hoaxes. This is going to cause the death of someone yet."

A team's self-sufficiency and ability to evacuate itself can mean life or death. Because of acclimatization problems, help from other parties is often nonexistent and helicopters, for many reasons, are not always available.

The National Park Service (NPS) has refused helicopter evacuations to climbers who can safely be taken down the mountain. If the victim is dying and the weather is good, it can still take many hours, or even days, for the NPS to find a suitable helicopter with a willing pilot. Helicopters do not stand by for Denali rescues and are often not insured for high-altitude landings. In the past, the NPS or the Army has paid the cost ($300–$13,000) of almost all rescues. However, it would be wise for climbers to obtain British or European insurance which will cover air evacuation costs. (It is possible the National Park Service will begin billing victims.)

Rescue Procedure

Safety should be foremost in every climber's mind while preparing for climbing Denali. The author believes that most rescues are the result of secondary, obsessive factors (such as reaching the summit) that overshadow the primary consideration of coming back unscathed.

The following procedure is recommended for rescue: treat the victim until his condition is stable; if possible move the victim to a lower elevation immediately; radio the NPS for a helicopter if the victim's condition is deteriorating rapidly, or radio the base camp caretaker or a bush pilot to arrange for air evacuation from the lowest point to which the victim can safely be moved.

APPROACHES

Glacier Flying

From the south, the usual approach is by ski plane from Talkeetna to the Southeast Fork of the Kahiltna Glacier or to the Ruth Glacier. However, some groups walk or ski in from the Anchorage-Fairbanks highway, a distance of about one hundred miles.

Buses, limousines, planes and a train operate between Anchorage and Talkeetna. In Talkeetna, there are air services that fly climbers to either side of the mountain. As of 1982, round-trip flights ranged from $200–$225 per person. To guarantee a prompt flight in, it is best to make a reservation in advance and place a deposit. Climbers can sometimes wait up to ten days for the weather to clear so that the pilots can fly. From early May until late July, there is a radio caretaker, employed by the pilots, on the Southeast Fork of the Kahiltna Glacier who coordinates Talkeetna-bound flights and monitors Channel 19 on the CB radio twenty-four hours a day.

In addition to the Talkeetna pilots, there is one air service that will fly climbers to Kantishna, for approaches up the Peters or Muldrow glaciers. (See Appendix M.)

Dog Sled Reference

From the north, the Peters or Muldrow Glacier can be approached on skis or by dog sled. (See Appendix M.)

WEATHER

There is a popular belief that the weather in Alaska changes very rapidly. Although there are elements of truth in this statement, it needs clarification. From a relatively clear sky, a violent storm can appear within two hours. In such cases, however, telltale signs are almost always visible several hours ahead. Such signs would include long cloud streaks in the sky and lenticular caps over the high summits. (The summit must be avoided when these lenticular caps are on it!) When the weather is really clear, it rarely turns bad in less than twelve hours. A completely good weather day has a noticeable brightness in the air which a day of changing weather usually doesn't have. Good and bad weather tends to come in cycles. Good weather can last three to six days while bad conditions of ten consecutive days are not unusual. During this bad weather period, there will be some temporary clearings. Heavy clouds at lower or higher elevations on other mountains will indicate that the bad weather may return. When it does return, the change in condition can be sudden. At low elevation, usually not above eight thousand feet, climbers may also be annoyed by clouds that hang not more than one thousand feet above the glacier. These clouds, which creep in off the ocean, bring whiteout and light rain or snow. They often appear when the weather higher on the mountain is excellent. These clouds, which are most common in July, can interfere with glacier flying and landings. It should be no surprise that wind will interfere with climbing more often than falling snow. If routes are marked with wands or if whiteout conditions aren't too bad, climbing can sometimes be done at low elevations even during snow storms. When the wind does blow, however, it can be very violent, possibly up to 100 mph at higher elevations. The prevailing wind will be from the south or southwest but currents around the mountain can create strong gusts from any direction.

Snowfall will be heavy during storms. One to two feet of

snow in a twenty-four-hour period or three feet in two days is not unusual. It is normal to have a short break for a few hours after three days of continuous snow but the storm can easily return after that break. Ten feet of powder snow in ten days is possible although this would consolidate into perhaps five feet of solid snow. In general, there is no such thing as a partly cloudy day. Either the sky is clear or it snows.

It is probable that every mountain could be climbed in any month of the year but some months are decidedly inhospitable for obvious reasons. Denali is one of the coldest mountains in the world because of its proximity to the Arctic Circle. From late April through August, it is not uncommon to experience temperatures of $-30°F$ with 100 mph winds, whiteouts and ground blizzards. Conversely, the temperature can reach 80°F with slush puddles on the glacier. Several factors are important in deciding on dates for an Alaskan expedition. These are: hours of daylight, prevailing weather trends, and temperature ranges.

Hours of Daylight

Between June 1 and July 15, there are nearly twenty-four hours of daylight in Alaska and the Yukon. The sun actually goes down for four hours but the twilight is usually bright enough for all-night climbing. This has two important advantages. It permits evening climbing when daytime climbing would be hazardous because of sun-induced avalanche conditions. It also permits the climber to begin and end his day whenever he wants and weather conditions permit. For example, if a storm ends at 2 P.M., the climber can then start to climb whereas, farther south, this day would be lost for climbing.

Before May 15 and after August 1, there are at least three hours of total darkness. Outside of this date range, storms will upset climbing schedules because the opportunity to climb throughout the night will not exist.

Prevailing Weather Trends

The prevailing winds are south and southwest off the ocean. The prevailing wind from the ocean usually carries warm air. When this warm air hits the glacier-surrounded mountains, precipitation follows. The warmer the temperature, the higher the probability of bad weather.

In the Denali area, there are likely to be a fair number of clear, but often cold and windy, days in April and early May. Although one hundred fifty miles from the ocean, Denali is unprotected from the sea to the south.

Thus, by the end of May, warm air from the ocean makes its way to Denali and local storms develop. The weather, particularly on the southern side where the clouds often boil up, gets progressively worse after July. September is a poor month, with the highest amount of precipitation in Alaska. In February and March, there are often long periods of cold, clear weather. However, there are also violent winds from the north in winter.

Temperature Ranges

It is possible for all of the big mountains to have very cold temperatures even in midsummer. Temperatures of −50°F have been recorded by climbers on Denali in June and July. The disadvantage of climbing in April is that, in spite of more clear days, the temperatures are colder. (From December–March, temperatures drop below −40°F for days on end and for twenty-four hours at a time.) As a rule of thumb, one can assume that the temperature will be three degrees colder for each one thousand feet of elevation. Air temperatures during the day at eight thousand feet in June and July average around 30°F. The air temperature will drop five to ten degrees during the evening, although the change will seem much greater if the sun has been shining. Temperatures inside tents at midday can reach 80°F because of the sun.

CLEAN CLIMBING

On the West Rib, the remains of a burned out tent are visible at 15,200 feet and human feces dot the snow both there and at the 16,500-foot campsite. In many places low on the Cassin, there are veritable tangles of old fixed line. At 16,500 feet, climbers have jettisoned excess weight

Crowds on the West Buttress route.

from their packs; looking around in the obvious, sheltered tent site, one can find assorted hardware, a new climbing rope, a pair of long underwear, books and various pieces of trash. Although much smaller, this site is similar to the 16,400-foot and 17,200-foot campsites on the West Buttress in that one must select cooking snow very carefully from among the wasteland of brown turds. Or, you can walk the Muldrow Glacier down low and find old canvas army tents, sardine cans and rotted clothing. On McGonagall Pass, the Sierra Club has initiated a trash cleanup trip.

Fortunately, Denali is huge and sometimes, below fifteen thousand feet, snowfall will cover the excrement, the bodies, the trash and the jettisoned gear. Up high on the mountain, where the wind blows away the snow cover, there is a permanent raised sidewalk from Denali Pass to the summit. Irreversible damage has been done. Every year the number of climbers on Denali increases. Human waste disposal is a health hazard at the more popular campsites. Like the number of climbers, the damage will continue to escalate, unless climbers behave thoughtfully.

Guidelines

Plan ahead about how to remove trash, food, fuel and all gear from the mountain. Expeditions prepared for every contingency with superfluous food, gear and gas will have a hard time getting it all down. Paper trash, such as toilet paper, can be burned but on properly planned, lightweight alpine-style climbs, it's easier to bring the trash down. All climbers should repack food and leave excess foil and paper wrappings at home. (Freeze-dried food does not spoil without foil wrappers.) Under the pretext of generosity to other climbers, caches are often abandoned. However, these caches inevitably become trash dumps. Whatever supplies are carried up must be carried or dragged back down.

Dig latrine pits eighteen to twenty-four inches deep and stake out large, heavy-duty plastic garbage bags with wands. Waste (feces, food scraps, ashes from burnt trash) can go into the bag; when the camp is broken, the bag should be thrown into the nearest deep crevasse. On steep routes, without crevasses, climbers must take care to drop feces away from campsite drinking snow and the route below. Fixed rope has to be pulled off the mountain after the climb. Expeditions should consult National Park Service Mountaineering Rangers about current waste problems before leaving for the mountains.

MEDICAL

Recommendations

Climbers must be prepared to give medical treatment and not just first aid. It is helpful to have a doctor or an emergency medical technician in each party. At the very least, everyone should be experienced in first aid. Team members should be aware of one another's medical problems and the side effects of various drugs.

Drug Side Effects

Sleeping pills are a respiratory depressant and can invite pulmonary edema. Tetracycline can increase an individual's sensitivity to the sun. Lasix is a diuretic which causes severe dehydration. Diamox is not generally accepted as a prophylactic for preventing altitude sickness; it also causes a tingling in the extremeties that is very similar to the sensation one gets with cold fingers or toes. When preparing medical kits, climbers should consult recent high-altitude medical literature. (Refer to Appendix N for medical kit suggestions.)

DIET

Arctic living conditions and vigorous exercise will raise the caloric demand of a climber on Denali to nearly double that of the average American. Fats (margarine, peanut butter, oil, cheese and nuts) are invaluable in combatting the cold. However, too many fats and all proteins are hard to digest and will hinder acclimatization above fourteen thousand feet where a high carbohydrate diet is recommended.

Six days of food should be left at base camp and fifteen to twenty-five days of food should be carried on the climb.

Menu

The expedition menu can make or break a trip. Freeze-dried food is good for quick, alpine-style climbs. It is light-weight and quick to cook but bland; a spice kit can help. At high altitude, the cooking time is longer (food sometimes has to be boiled in a pot rather than soaked) and it can be unpalatable.

There are many inexpensive dried foods (rice, pasta, cereals) that are as light as freeze-dried food, more nutritious and easy to prepare. Down low on the mountain, meat, eggs, canned fruits and cheesecake can do wonders for morale. Fresh food freezes and spoils. Some groups carry whole grains and a pressure cooker which minimizes cooking time and fuel consumption. Regardless of the menu, spartan diets are not advised, since food becomes a central, coveted item on Denali.

Fluids

Rehydration is the most important part of one's diet on Denali. Fluid loss from the body is high due to strenuous exercise in the dry air. Drinking four quarts of fluid each day can help prevent altitude sickness, exhaustion and frostbite. Diuretics, such as coffee or caffeinated tea, should be avoided. Cocoa, herbal tea, milk and soup are all fine. Thermoses containing hot drinks are marvelous for restoring energy on cold climbing days. Water and sugar drinks should be carried in a properly insulated one- to two-quart container (some climbers have become dehydrated during the day because their water has frozen).Generally speaking, if the urine is not gin clear and regular, the climber is dehydrated and should be drinking more.

GROUP EQUIPMENT

Tents: The most popular, practical tent on Denali is the three-man Dome tent. For comfort, however, some parties use the high-profile McKinley tent which doesn't hold up well in high winds. Other climbers save weight and sacrifice living space by using various types of tunnel tents that stand up in high winds and are good for small bivouac sites on the steeper routes. Dark-colored tents induce depression during long storm periods. A whisk broom and sponge should be allotted to each tent for cleaning out snow and spills. Most tent sites will be located on snow where ordinary snowstakes sometimes work and where ice axes, snow pickets, flukes, wands, skis, ski poles and snowshoes all work well.

Stoves: As melting water is an essential part of a Denali climb, careful attention must be given to the choice of a stove. To minimize the possibility of tent fires and repair problems, climbers should use the stove they are most familiar with. (In 1980, a party on the West Rib had a harrowing experience when their tent burned down because they were unfamiliar with a flare-up problem on their stove.)

In order of their popularity on Denali, climbers use white gas, butane or kerosene stoves. The writer's preference is the MSR white gas stove. Most any part can be repaired but, like other combustible gas stoves, it should be used outside as much as possible. Unless a piece of asbestos is added, the heat at the bottom of the stove will melt whatever material it is placed on. The stove is light, fuel efficient and boils water faster than any other stove.

Mike Covington uses Optimus 001 kerosene stoves on Denali. Kerosene is not combustible and is not as dangerous as white gas stoves. Although the fumes can be bothersome, these stoves can be used safely inside of well-ventilated tents. One drawback, however, is that the burner orifice on this stove has to be pricked regularly. The boiling time is somewhat slower than on the MSR and, if the fuel supply is depleted, it is unlikely that other parties will have any kerosene to loan. Both kerosene and white gas stoves require a preheating fuel or paste.

Some climbers, like Peter Metcalf and Glenn Randall,

prefer renovated Bluet butane cannister stoves. With a good windscreen and copper tubing from the burner to an insulated cartridge nest as a heat exchange, this stove, which is spillproof, can be hung from the tent ceiling, thus freeing floor space. To prevent possible flareups and to increase the heat output, the stove and cartridges should be prewarmed under jackets or in sleeping bags for ten minutes. Once the stove has warmed up, the boiling time is nearly equal to the MSR. This stove is also quiet, which is a godsend during the dinner hour. However, climbers who choose to use this stove on Denali should carefully consider the matter of carrying the disposable cartridges back down.

With any type of stove, pocket lighters are invaluable. Insulation beneath the stove and windscreens is essential. One stove will do for up to three people. With all stoves, the hazards of tent fires and carbon monoxide poisoning from improper ventilation must be recognized.

Fuel: For kerosene or gas stoves, the minimum consumption—for freeze-dried food, not allowing any extra for burning trash—is one quarter pint per person per day. The minimum consumption for Butane stoves, for freeze-dried food, is one large Bluet butane cannister per person for three days. A two-person team on a three-week climb would carry thirteen butane cannisters or three one-quart Sigg bottles with gas or kerosene. Gas and kerosene can also be carried in one-gallon, square-sided fuel containers. Fuel containers must be tested for leaks. It is important that they be kept separate from food to prevent contamination.

Pots: Two nesting cook pots, from one and a half to two and a half quarts, are recommended for each cooking group.

Ropes: The optimal climbing rope is the 165-foot, 9mm Everdry. On technical routes, climbers sometimes use 300-foot, 9mm ropes. Since 1976, the major routes on Denali have been done alpine style without using fixed ropes. Some routes are still done in the old, seige style and, unfortunately, abandoned ropes and hardware often litter them. Although fixed-rope climbing allows for better acclimatization, it also entails a longer exposure to objective dangers and a considerable increase in work. The simplest solution is to consider an alpine-style ascent of a route that is within the team's abilities.

Parachute or alpine cord in 100- to 200-foot lengths is invaluable and can be used for innumerable repairs.

Snow shovels with large, sturdy aluminum scoops are essential for digging out tents during storms and for digging latrines, snow caves and cooking shelters. Plastic avalanche shovels are too small and will break.

Snow saws are needed to block walls around tents or to build igloos.

Plastic bags are always in demand. Ten large, heavy-duty garbage bags should be carried for latrines.

Spare parts should be considered for ice axes, crampons, tents (poles), stoves, skis, snowshoes and shovels.

Tool and repair kit should be carried for fixing ice axes, crampons, tents, stoves, skis, snowshoes, shovels, sleds and clothing. Such a kit might include: mechanic's wire, duct tape, hose clamps, file, crescent wrench, pliers, screwdriver, glue, wrench, and needle and thread.

Miscellaneous gear: Pot grips, scouring pads and toilet paper.

Thermometer authenticates the war stories when you get home.

Climbing hardware varies according to the difficulty of the route. The minimum amount, sufficient for the West Buttress or Muldrow Glacier, is one ice screw (or snow-fluke) and one ice ax per person for crevasse rescue.

Radio: The National Park Service recommends that all parties carry a radio. Although there is no doubt that they have saved lives, it is not known how many parties depend on radios or rescues rather than prudence and self-sufficiency. There are, however, climbers who regard climbing Denali as a wilderness experience, in which they are isolated from the outside world and must depend only on their own resources.

Five-watt CB radios are those most commonly used. Channel 19 is monitored by the radio caretaker at the Southeast Fork of the Kahiltna, by Talkeetna glacier pilots, the National Park Service and various people living in the Alaska bush. FM transceivers are used to transmit to telephone operators in Anchorage and Fairbanks. Since there are few CB monitors on the north side of the mountain, an FM transceiver is recommended. Both CB and FM units are line-of-sight and are generally effective only above fourteen thousand feet. Both radios are fairly light. Several sets of batteries should be carried. (See Appendix O.)

For use on routes like the Wickersham or the Northwest Buttress, there are sideband radios which can transmit nonline-of-sight or below fourteen thousand feet. An extra sideband radio must be left with the base camp caretaker or a bush pilot so that the party can be monitored.

Signal devices such as smoke flares, emergency locator transmitters and rocket flares might be carried as radio communication is not always possible or desirable. There is no guarantee, however, that the weather will permit signalling. Air-to-ground signal arrangements should be made with the Park Service or pilots.

PERSONAL EQUIPMENT

Boots: Vapor barrier ("mouse") boots are fine for the West Buttress or Muldrow Glacier routes. Plastic double boots are best for technical routes.

Overboots are needed for any type of double boot. They must be well insulated in the sole.

Gaitors are essential on vapor barrier boots and are more comfortable for double boots when down low on the mountain.

171

Twelve-point crampons must fit snugly with allowance for overboots. Strapless (Footfang) or cable-binding crampons are good in extreme cold.

Socks: At least two changes of wool socks should be carried.

Vapor barrier socks can reduce the number of wool socks carried. Both socks and feet must be dried every night to prevent immersion foot.

T-shirt: This is useful on the hot, lower glaciers.

Polypropelene underwear takes perspiration away from the skin to the next layer of clothing. Tops and bottoms are suggested.

Expedition underwear: Wool, Damart or Patagonia tops and bottoms all work well.

Mountain pants: Pile, wool, thinsulate or fiberfill pants should be ankle length.

Wind pants: Gore-Tex is best, although regular, breathable nylon will work too. Bibs are warmer and keep the snow out better.

Hooded windjacket should be Gore-Tex and fit loosely.

Pile jacket is indispensable and works well as a pillow.

Hooded down jacket is great around camp, on bivouacs or on summit days.

Wool shirt can be worn underneath the pile jacket.

Patagonia polypropelene gloves seem to outwear any other gloves. Bring two pair.

Helly Hansen pile or Dachstein wool mittens dry out quicker than any other mittens. Bring two pair.

Overmitts should be made out of Cordura; Gore-Tex seems to wear out too quickly. Idiot straps prevent the mitten system from getting lost.

Balaclava made out of pile or wool is essential.

Silk mask is nice when it gets very cold.

Spare wool hat should be carried for each party.

Face masks with eye slits tend to blind the wearer. Half-neoprene ski Masques work well in conjunction with goggles.

Goggles work well in blowing snow conditions but are prone to fogging. Only lenses that screen out ultraviolet light should be used.

Mountaineering glasses should screen out at least ninety percent of the ultraviolet light radiation. Side shields are necessary. A spare pair of glasses should be carried.

Visored cap is important for sun protection.

Water bottle should have a one- to two-quart capacity. Water will freeze if the bottle is not properly insulated.

Pack with soft internal frame is preferred by most climbers, although heavier loads are easier to carry with an external frame pack. External frames are a hindrance for technical climbing or skiing.

Ice ax should have a safety strap (attached to the wrist or harness), otherwise a spare ax should be carried. Technical routes demand an ax shorter than seventy centimeters. For the Muldrow or West Buttress routes an ax under sixty-five centimeters would be too short.

Helmets are necessary only on technical routes.

Ascenders, such as Jumars, Clogs or Gibbs, are mandatory and should be attached to the rope at all times. Gibbs work best on iced ropes.

Ice screw or snow fluke, either one or both, should be carried by each climber for crevasse rescue.

Climbing harness is essential.

Sleeping bags made of fiberfill or down both work well. Fiberfill is heavier than down but is preferable for warmth when wet. Although there are usually enough sunny days to dry out a down sleeping bag, it should be used with a bivouac cover or be made out of Gore-Tex.

Vapor barrier liner can add ten degrees of warmth to the sleeping bag as well as keeping it dry. It is an inexpensive, lightweight item.

Sleeping pad must be at least one-half inch thick; some climbers carry two. It is important to get a brand that will not freeze and break in the cold. Thermarests are great but a puncture would be a let down. Without a pad, a sleeping bag is nearly useless.

Skis or snowshoes speed glacier travel, which would be much slower and more dangerous without them. Skins are recommended for skis. Sherpa brand snowshoes are light and sturdy.

Sled or haul bag inside a tube tent makes transporting gear on a glacier much easier than if it were all carried inside a pack. Sleds will tip over unless they are expensive, custom-made models. Cheap plastic tube tents covering a haul bag work great. Fasten the tube tent at both ends, like a giant sausage, then tie the dragline into a swivel gate attached to the haul bag. The tube tent can roll over sideways without having to be righted and without tangling the rope.

Pocket knife is invaluable.

Eating bowl, cup and spoon, as well as journal, pencil, camera and film, are other important items to carry.

Books and other reading material become quite popular during bad weather. Each book should be of general interest. It is questionable whether German language poetry or physics qualify as general interest reading. Books emphasizing sex and violence always seem to be popular.

APPENDICES

Appendix A

NUMBER OF CLIMBERS ATTEMPTING DENALI 1903–1982

YEARS	NUMBER OF CLIMBERS	REACHED SUMMIT
1903–1912	42	0
1913–1922	4	4
1923–1932	13	4
1933–1942	18	7
1943–1952	44	21
1953–1962	167	98
1963–1972	802	406
1973–1977	1715	1001
1978–1982	2959	1535
80-YEAR TOTAL	5764	3076

Appendix B

ASCENT–DESCENT INCIDENT
AND FATALITY RATES ON DENALI
1903–1982

INCIDENTS

CATEGORY	NUMBER OF INCIDENTS	PERCENT
ASCENT	102	69.39
DESCENT	45	30.61

FATALITIES

CATEGORY	NUMBER OF CLIMBERS	PERCENT
ASCENT	14	34.15
DESCENT	27	65.85

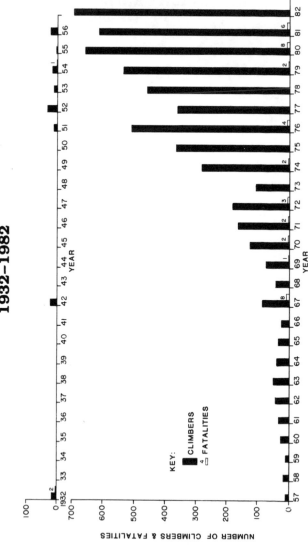

Appendix C

ANNUAL SUMMARY OF CLIMBERS AND FATALITIES ON DENALI
1932–1982

Appendix D
FATALITIES ON DENALI
1903–1982

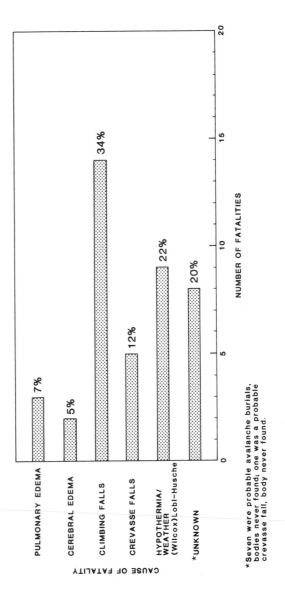

*Seven were probable avalanche burials, bodies never found; one was a probable crevasse fall, body never found.

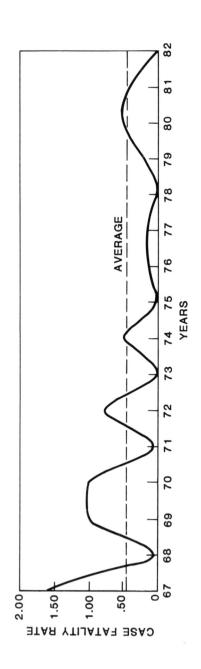

Appendix E

CASE FATALITY RATE ON DENALI
COMPARISON OF
FATALITIES WITH ACCIDENTS
1967–1982

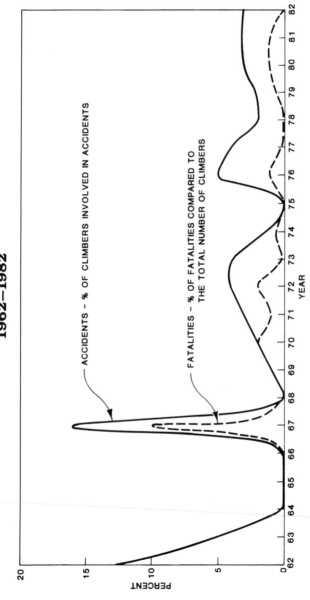

Appendix F

ANNUAL ACCIDENT AND FATALITY RATES ON DENALI 1962–1982

ACCIDENTS – % OF CLIMBERS INVOLVED IN ACCIDENTS

FATALITIES – % OF FATALITIES COMPARED TO THE TOTAL NUMBER OF CLIMBERS

Appendix G
REPORTED ACCIDENTS ON DENALI
1903–1982

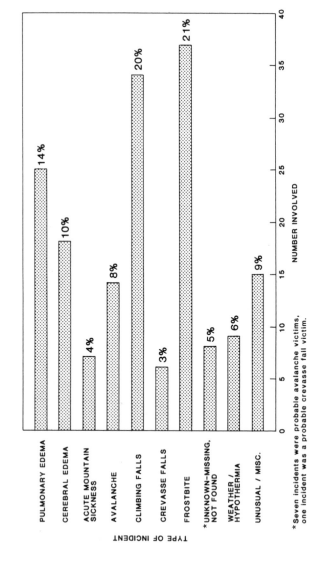

*Seven incidents were probable avalanche victims, one incident was a probable crevasse fall victim.

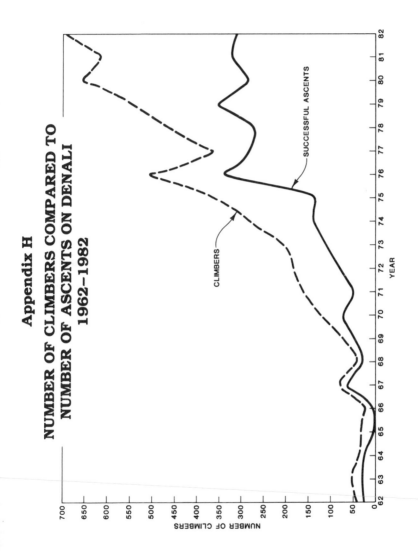

Appendix H
NUMBER OF CLIMBERS COMPARED TO NUMBER OF ASCENTS ON DENALI
1962–1982

Appendix I

DENALI CASE INCIDENT
RATE BY NATIONALITY
1903–1982

NATIONALITY	NUMBER OF CLIMBERS	INVOLVED IN INCIDENT	PERCENT
U.S. AMERICAN	4037	114	2.82
JAPANESE	725	21	2.89
GERMAN	238	15	6.30
SWISS	148	8	5.41
CANADIAN	125	8	6.40
FRENCH	107	1	0.93
AUSTRIAN	83	3	3.61
BRITISH	60	6	10.00
SPANISH	34	1	2.94
KOREAN	33	3	9.09
ITALIAN	28	3	10.71
SCOTTISH	13	1	7.69
SWEDISH	10	1	10.00
CZECH	5	3	60.00

Appendix J

GUIDE SERVICES AUTHORIZED TO OPERATE IN DENALI NATIONAL PARK AND PRESERVE

Concessionaire Permit

Aerie Northwest
7415 Meridian Avenue North
Seattle, Washington 98103
206-524-5002

Genet Expeditions
Talkeetna, Alaska 99676
907-733-2414

American Alpine Institute
1212 24th Street
Bellingham, Washington 98225
206-671-1505

Fantasy Ridge Mountain Guides
P.O. Box 206
Woody Creek, Colorado 81656
303-925-9581

Mountain Trip
P.O. Box 41161
Anchorage, Alaska 99509
907-345-6499

Rainier Mountaineering, Inc.
201 St. Helens Avenue
Tacoma, Washington 98402
206-627-6242

Educational Permit

National Outdoor Leadership School
P.O. Box AA
Lander, Wyoming 82520
307-332-6973

Appendix K

INFORMATION SOURCES
FOR EXPEDITIONS TO DENALI

Journals

Accidents in North American Mountaineering
The American Alpine Journal
The American Alpine Club
113 East 90th Street
New York, New York 10128

The Canadian Alpine Journal
The Alpine Club of Canada
P.O. Box 1026
Banff, Alberta T0L 0C0
Canada

The Mountain World
Published by the Swiss Foundation for Alpine Research from
1953 to 1969. Collections available for reference in the library of
the American Alpine Club and serveral other libraries which
have mountaineering collections.

Magazines

Climbing
P.O. Box E
Aspen, Colorado 81612

Mountain
P.O. Box 184
Sheffield S11 9DL
England

Summit
P.O. Box 1889
Big Bear Lake, California 92315

Map of Mount McKinley

Boston's Museum of Science
Science Park
Boston, Massachusetts 02114

Photographs

In addition to the photographs listed in Appendix L, other Washburn photographs of Denali routes are available. For further information and prices, write to:

Boston's Museum of Science
Attention: Bradford Washburn
Science Park
Boston, Massachusetts 02114
617-723-2500

Avalanche Information

American Avalanche Institute
P.O. Box 308
Wilson, Wyoming 83014

Expedition Information

Denali National Park and Preserve
P.O. Box 9
Denali National Park, Alaska 99755

Appendix L

COMPARATIVE RATING OF ROUTES ON DENALI

ROUTE	RATING	FIRST ASCENT	WASHBURN PHOTO NO.*
MULDROW GLACIER	EASY-MODERATE	1913	3220, 3287
WEST BUTTRESS	EASY-MODERATE	1951	7267, 7233, 5048
PIONEER RIDGE	MODERATE	1961	7166, 4274
WICKERSHAM WALL (West Rim)	MODERATE (Avalanche danger)	1963	4417, 4424
SOUTH BUTTRESS (Thayer Basin)	MODERATE	1954	5040, 5867, 5847, 5171, 3090
NORTHWEST BUTTRESS	HARD	1954	4418, 5031
WEST RIB	HARD	1959	5060, 4781
MESSNER COULOIR	HARD	1976	4795
SOUTH BUTTRESS (Japanese Variation)	HARD	1965	4039
SOUTHEAST SPUR	HARD	1962	5172, 7013, 7867
EAST BUTTRESS	HARD	1963	5206, 5211
WICKERSHAM WALL (Direct)	DIFFICULT	1963	4424, 4827
CASSIN RIDGE	DIFFICULT	1961	5168, 5180, 5980
SOUTHEAST SPUR (Southwest Leg)	DIFFICULT	1975	3063, 5137
SOUTHWEST FACE	VERY DIFFICULT	1980	5050, 4782
AMERICAN DIRECT (South Face)	VERY DIFFICULT	1967	5054, 5981, 4930
AMERICAN DIRECT (Scott-Haston Variation)	VERY DIFFICULT	1976	5799, 5055
CZECH (South Face)	VERY DIFFUCULT	1980	5981, 5054, 4930
SOUTHEAST WALL (Isis Face)	VERY DIFFICULT	1982	5137
SOUTHEAST WALL (Unnamed & unclimbed as of 1982)	VERY DIFFICULT		5869, 5872

*See Appendix K

Appendix M

DENALI
APPROACH SERVICES

Air Service

The following air services will fly climbers to Denali:

Hudson Air Service, Inc.
Main Street
Talkeetna, Alaska 99676
907-733-2321

K2 Aviation
P.O. Box 290
Talkeetna, Alaska 99676
907-733-2291

Talkeetna Air Taxi
P.O. Box 73
Talkeetna, Alaska 99676
907-733-2218

The following air service will fly climbers to Kantishna for approaches up the Peters and Muldrow glaciers:

Denali Wilderness Air
P.O. Box 82
Denali National Park, Alaska 99755
907-683-2261

Dog Sled Service

Denali Dog Tours & Wilderness Freighters
P.O. Box 1
Denali National Park, Alaska 99755

Appendix N

MEDICAL KIT SUGGESTIONS FOR EXPEDITIONS TO DENALI

ITEM	USE
CODEINE	PAINKILLER
CORICIDIN	FOR COLDS
DEMEROL	STRONG PAINKILLER
DIAMOX	POSSIBLE AMS PREVENTION
HEMORRHOID OINTMENT	HEMORRHOID INFLAMMATION
HYDROCORTISONE EYE OINTMENT	SNOWBLINDNESS
KEFLEX	ANTIBIOTIC
LABIOSAN	LIP PROTECTION
LASIX	HAPE OR HACE
LOMOTIL	DIARRHEA
PENICILLIN	ANTIBIOTIC
SUNBLOCK	SUNBURN PREVENTION
VALIUM	MUSCLE RELAXANT, MILD SLEEP AID

Additional items which might be included:

GAUZE SUTURE KIT
COMPRESSES ADHESIVE TAPE
RECTAL THERMOMETER SPARE SUNGLASSES

Two books are recommended as valuable field guides:

Mountain Sickness, by Peter H. Hackett, M.D., The American Alpine Club, New York

Medicine for Mountaineering, by James A. Wilkerson, M.D., The Mountaineers, Seattle

Appendix O

RADIO INFORMATION SOURCES
FOR EXPEDITIONS TO DENALI

Alaska Mountaineering & Hiking
2633 Spenard Road
Anchorage, Alaska 99503
907-272-1811

Alaska Mountaineering & Hiking
Talkeetna, Alaska 99676
907-733-2526

McCaw Telepage
4797 Business Park Boulevard – #2
Anchorage, Alaska 99503
907-562-2772

Communications Equipment & Service Company
1010 College Road
Fairbanks, Alaska 99701
907-452-1049

BIBLIOGRAPHY

Davidson, Art. *Minus 148°: The Winter Ascent of Mt. McKinley.* W.W. Norton & Company Inc., New York, 1969.

Hackett, Peter H. *Mountain Sickness: Prevention, Recognition & Treatment.* The American Alpine Club, New York, 1980.

Heath, Donald and David Reid Williams. *Man at High Altitude: The Pathophysiology of Acclimatization and Adaptation.* Churchill Livingstone, Edinburgh, 1977.

Houston, Charles S. *Going High: The Story of Man and Altitude.* Charles S. Houston, Burlington (Vermont) and The American Alpine Club, New York, 1980.

Jones, Chris. *Climbing in North America.* University of California Press, Berkeley and The American Alpine Club, New York, 1976.

Mills, W.J. "Frostbite and Hypothermia." *Alaska Medicine,* March 1973.

Moore, Terris. *Mt. McKinley: The Pioneer Climbs.* University of Alaska Press, College, 1967.

Mountaineering: Denali National Park and Preserve, Alaska. National Park Service, U.S. Department of the Interior, 1983.

Perla, Ronald I. and M. Martinelli, Jr. *Avalanche Handbook.* Forest Service, U.S. Department of Agriculture, Agriculture Handbook 489. Fort Collins (Colorado), 1976.

Snyder, Howard H. *The Hall of the Mountain King.* Charles Scribner's Sons, New York, 1973.

Stuck, Hudson. *The Ascent of Denali (Mount McKinley): A Narrative of the First Complete Ascent of the Highest Peak in North America.* Charles Scribner's Sons, New York, 1914.

Washburn, Bradford. *Frostbite.* (Reprint from 1962 *American Alpine Journal.*) The Museum of Science, Boston.

Wilcox, Joe. *White Winds.* Hwong Publishing Company, Los Alamitos (California), 1981.

Wilkerson, James A., editor. *Medicine for Mountaineering,* 2nd edition. The Mountaineers, Seattle, 1975.

Wilson, Rodman et al. "Death on Denali." *Western Journal of Medicine,* June 1978.